Successful Job Applications

Teach Yourself®

Patricia Scudamore
and Hilton Catt

www.inaweek.co.uk

KT-364-068

Hodder Education

338 Euston Road, London NW1 3BH.

Hodder Education is an Hachette UK company

First published in UK 2003 by Hodder Education

First published in US 2012 by The McGraw-Hill Companies, Inc.

This edition published 2012.

Copyright © 2003, 2012 Patricia Scudamore and Hilton Catt

The moral rights of the author have been asserted

A previous edition of this book was published by Hodder in 2003.

Database right Hodder Education (makers)

The *Teach Yourself* name is a registered trademark of Hachette UK.

All rights reserved. No part of this publication may be reproduced, stored in a retrieval system or transmitted in any form or by any means, electronic, mechanical, photocopying, recording or otherwise, without the prior permission in writing of Hodder Education, or as expressly permitted by law, or under terms agreed with the appropriate reprographic rights organization. Enquiries concerning reproduction outside the scope of the above should be sent to the Rights Department, Hodder Education, at the address above.

You must not circulate this book in any other binding or cover and you must impose this same condition on any acquirer.

British Library Cataloguing in Publication Data: a catalogue record for this title is available from the British Library.

Library of Congress Catalog Card Number: on file.

The publisher has used its best endeavours to ensure that any website addresses referred to in this book are correct and active at the time of going to press. However, the publisher and the author have no responsibility for the websites and can make no guarantee that a site will remain live or that the content will remain relevant, decent or appropriate.

The publisher has made every effort to mark as such all words which it believes to be trademarks. The publisher should also like to make it clear that the presence of a word in the book, whether marked or unmarked, in no way affects its legal status as a trademark.

Every reasonable effort has been made by the publisher to trace the copyright holders of material in this book. Any errors or omissions should be notified in writing to the publisher, who will endeavour to rectify the situation for any reprints and future editions.

Hachette UK's policy is to use papers that are natural, renewable and recyclable products and made from wood grown in sustainable forests. The logging and manufacturing processes are expected to conform to the environmental regulations of the country of origin.

www.hoddereducation.co.uk

Typeset by Cenveo Publisher Services.

Printed in Great Britain by CPI Group (UK) Ltd, Croydon, CR0 4YY

Successful Job Applications
In A Week

Patricia Scudamore and Hilton Catt

EAST SUSSEX COUNTY COUNCIL
WITHDRAWN

0 7 JUN 2024

17

The Teach Yourself series has been trusted around the world for over 60 years. This series of 'In A Week' business books is designed to help people at all levels and around the world to further their careers. Learn in a week, what the experts learn in a lifetime.

04068720

Patricia Scudamore and Hilton Catt have operated in the employment field for many years. They run their own business, the Scudamore Catt Partnership. They have written a number of books on career management, including other titles in this series.

Contents

Introduction   2

Sunday   4
Defining the task

Monday   18
You and the image you present

Tuesday   32
Selection criteria

Wednesday   46
Getting interviews

Thursday   64
Going for interviews

Friday   82
Handling questions

Saturday   100
In the last few

Surviving in tough times   116

Answers   121

Introduction

Teach yourself in a week everything you need to know about job applications and how to make them work. Starting on Sunday and going through to Saturday, learn the stages of a job application step by step so you build up a picture of what it takes to:

● keep your applications moving from one stage to the next
● bring them to successful conclusions.

A central message in the book is the importance of being 'employer friendly', by which we mean understanding where employers are coming from and laying a path for them – a path favourable to you, of course.

For many job applicants, what goes on behind employers' closed doors remains a hidden world but, by Saturday, you will have taught yourself how job applications are processed, what employers look for when they make up interview lists and then, from the candidates they interview, who:

● to short-list
● to offer the job to.

Teach yourself most of all to consider what employers want and, at the same time, to consider how you could meet their needs. From this piece of simple analysis you will be able to formulate a plan for:

● what needs to go into your CV
● what you need to put in any letters of application you write
● what you need to say about yourself on any application forms you are asked to fill in.

Teach yourself today to consider that the way you go about applying for jobs depends to a large extent on how much competition you are up against. Where the competition is tough, getting an interview will be harder than where you are one of only a few applicants (where it would not be unusual to find that everyone is seen). Teach yourself how to measure competition and, where it looks like there will be large numbers of other applicants for the job, teach yourself how to make sure your name, and not someone else's, is on the interview list.

Teach yourself today that when you get to an interview you have a new task to face. Teach yourself the importance of getting the right messages across to the person or persons sitting on the other side of the desk and what the right messages are. Go one step further and teach yourself how to dictate the agenda for interviews so you will be on territory that is familiar to you and where the best parts of your application will come out.

Teach yourself, too, how to handle the awkward questions that some interviewers like to ask. Teach yourself to see what's behind the questions and what answers will impress the interviewer most.

Finally, this week teach yourself what to do when you get on a short-list (the final interview stage). Teach yourself how important it is to build on what you have done so far and how to keep up the good work. Teach yourself how to steer your job application over the last hurdle and on to the outcome you want, which is an offer of a job in your hands.

SUNDAY

Defining the task

Teach yourself today how the job market works and what employers do when they have positions to fill. Teach yourself the different methods they use and why. Teach yourself how, as a consequence of these different methods of recruiting staff, the job market has become divided into two sectors – the visible and the invisible.

Teach yourself that, in simple terms, the visible market is the jobs that are advertised whereas the invisible market is those that are not. Teach yourself today that the visible market is where you will face competition in the shape of other applicants who have seen the same advertisement as you and decided to give it a shot. Contrast the visible market with the invisible market where the challenge is not other candidates but finding out about the jobs in the first place.

Teach yourself today about the different selection procedures that employers use, ranging from the formal to the informal and how to handle both. Teach yourself today the importance of taking control of job applications so it's you sitting in the driving seat when it comes to moving them forward to successful conclusions.

How employers fill positions

ABC Industries want to appoint a manager to head up a new venture and, having decided they have no internal candidates to promote, their thoughts turn to finding someone suitable on the outside job market. How do they proceed? In terms of recruitment methods, what choices are open to them?

Advertising

Advertising is the traditional way to find staff. Put an advertisement in a newspaper or a publication, such as a trade magazine or professional journal, and see who applies.

Advertising today includes advertising on websites. Advertising is what everyone is familiar with.

Approach

ABC Industries may know people who would be suitable for their position – people they could make contact with (e.g. people who work for competitors). Alternatively, ABC could hire the services of a professional head-hunter (someone whose business it is to have contacts).

Recruitment consultants

Agencies or recruitment consultants keep details of candidates on file and, if ABC wanted to, they could ask a firm of recruitment consultants to do a file search and see which candidates match their specification.

Selecting recruiting methods

Employers tend to have preferences when it comes to recruiting methods. These are often based on their previous experience of what works and what doesn't. Here are three examples:

Company D

'We are a knowledge-based business and we tend to look for people with very defined and specialist skills. We find that the only way to recruit such people is through firms of specialist recruitment consultants.'

Company E

'We aim for the widest possible choice of candidates. This is why we always advertise our positions.'

Company F

'We work in a tight-knit industry, where everyone knows everyone else. When it comes to recruiting staff, we simply put the word round the trade and wait to see who comes forward.'

The visible and invisible job markets

What emerges from this quick overview of recruitment methods is that the job market can be split into two sectors.

The visible sector is there for everyone to see. It consists of jobs advertised either by employers or through firms of consultants. You access it by keeping your eyes open.

The invisible sector is harder to penetrate. It includes, for example, positions filled by approach or by employers tapping into consultants' databases. Getting into the invisible market means being proactive. You need, for instance, to get yourself known by putting your networking skills into practice. You have to get your name on the files of the right consultants.

Competition and how it arises

When you apply for a job, you have to first of all assess how much competition you will be up against. How do you do this? A useful measure of competition is to think about how you sourced the job. Did you see it advertised in a national newspaper, for example? If this is the case, you can safely assume that many other people will apply. Alternatively, did you source the job by putting out a few feelers in the trade in which you work? Here, the competition could be negligible or non-existent. You could even find yourself the only runner in a one-horse race.

> Moving your applications from one stage to the next has different connotations, depending on which sector of the job market you happen to be operating in. Visible market applications need to be focused on the task of engaging and overcoming competition, whereas the challenge you face with the invisible or unadvertised market is to keep the process you have started flowing.

Selection procedures

Selection procedures vary enormously. At one extreme, you could be asked along for a friendly chat, culminating in a job offer. At the other extreme, you could be in for a series of nail-biting grillings, backed up by psychological tests.

Are these variances completely random? Or is there some way of telling in advance what kind of selection procedure you will have to go through and what kind of ordeal you should prepare yourself for?

Although there is an element of unpredictability about selection procedures (employers please themselves), the following checklist gives a rough guide of what to expect:

Checklist

● Seniority. Are you applying for a top job (e.g. director or senior manager)? If so, expect to be put through the hoops.
● Size of organization. As a natural feature, bigger employers tend to have more formal selection procedures. Small firms, however, tend to be more relaxed in their approach.

- Professional involvement. Where consultants or human resources management professionals are involved, there will always be a tendency towards a more formalized and structured approach. For instance, interview with professionals first, followed by a short-list and re-interview by the manager who has responsibility for making the appointment. Note: involvement of professionals also ties in with the size of organizations – big firms are more likely to use professionals than their smaller counterparts.
- Competition. Where there are large numbers of applicants, the need will arise for some kind of sifting process. Candidates will probably face a series of selection stages with some candidates disposed of at each stage. Competition is often a feature of jobs that are advertised (visible market).

Designing strategies to address the task

It is clear that there is no one standard way to approach every job application. For example, psyching yourself up and rehearsing all sorts of smart answers to difficult interview questions will have little point if the person sitting on the other side of the desk is someone who has known you for the past 20 years. Similarly, taking a casual, laid-back approach will not earn you many brownie points if your application has to be vetted by an up-market firm of selection consultants.

Taking control

Taking control is important. It is about taking responsibility for moving your applications in the directions that you want them to go. Taking control means:

● not leaving the responsibility to others
● not leaving anything to chance.

Selection today

Selection, done properly, calls for commitment of time and resources.

For example, Company D want to recruit a project manager. They decide, therefore:

● to run an advertisement in the local evening newspaper
● to ask three firms of recruitment consultants to search their files and put suitable candidates forward.

The tasks for Company D break down as follows:

● putting together a job specification
● using the job specification to brief the firms of recruitment consultants
● preparing the advertisement
● handling the response (acknowledging letters, emails, phone calls, etc., sending out application forms)
● reading candidates' applications and CVs
● setting up and carrying out preliminary interviews
● re-interviewing the short-list
● general administration (e.g. jobs such as advising unsuccessful candidates and dealing with travelling expenses, etc.).

This list means that someone at Company D is going to be very busy. Moreover, since the someone in question is probably a senior manager with all sorts of other conflicting demands on his or her time, it is likely that the recruitment exercise will not be as well co-ordinated as it ought to be.

In their desire to cut costs, most businesses have been through various phases of headcount slashing in recent years. One of the side-effects has been a vast reduction in the number of administrative and support staff that businesses carry. The result is that more and more work is concentrated into fewer and fewer pairs of hands. Hence, the cracks start to appear very quickly when activities like selection assignments come up – activities that call for concentrated time and effort. They get done but they are not done as well as they might be and one of the manifestations of this is the large number of applications that go unanswered. To the outsider it seems like a case of bad manners. However, the usual explanation is that organizations with insufficient resources cannot get their acts together.

Getting in the driving seat

Given the circumstances that surround much selection in modern job market conditions (circumstances that can and do descend into the shambolic), there are enormous benefits for candidates who can take control of events and the pace at which they move. For instance, you can take control when a head-hunter promises to get back to you by saying 'I'd rather ring you' – use the excuse that it is difficult for you to talk at work. The advantage? You are in control. You can keep tabs on the head-hunter and make sure that their mind is focused on keeping your face in the frame. Conversely, you will avoid situations where you hear nothing and do not know what to make of it.

'Don't ring me, I'll ring you' is what employers used to say. Today it is you, the candidate, who should be saying this.

Steer job applications to successful outcomes

The immediate deduction to be made from all of this is that job applications should not be left to go off in their own directions.

They need steering and they need you to keep a firm grip on the wheel. Consequently, as part of defining the task in front of you when you apply for a job, you should take account of what lies on the road ahead. You should see the straight stretches where you can put your foot down. You should identify where you may have to get into a different gear to struggle up the hills. At the same time, you should learn to heed the warning signs. Never let your attention wander because this is where the danger lies.

Summary

Today you have taught yourself how the job market works and where, as an applicant, you fit in. From this appreciation you have seen that, with some jobs, there will be other candidates who will be interested in the job, not just you (the numbers can go into hundreds and thousands). With other jobs, however, you will not face the same challenges. Getting an interview will not be such an issue.

Today you have also taught yourself the different selection procedures that employers use and how it is usually possible to work out what hoops you are going to be put through. You should never take anything for granted of course. At one extreme, you could be in for a lengthy, drawn-out process, stretching over a number of weeks; at the other, you could be called in for a friendly chat where, at the end, you are told that the job is yours.

Finally, today you have taught yourself how important it is to take control of job applications so that you keep the process moving towards the outcome you want.

SUNDAY
MONDAY
TUESDAY
WEDNESDAY
THURSDAY
FRIDAY
SATURDAY

Fact-check (answers at the back)

1. What is the invisible job market?
   a) Jobs no one applies for ❑
   b) Jobs that don't exist ❑
   c) Jobs that are not advertised ❑
   d) Jobs you only find on websites ❑

2. Where will you face most competition?
   a) Visible market ❑
   b) Invisible market ❑
   c) Both the same ❑
   d) Jobs that don't ask for many qualifications ❑

3. What is approach?
   a) Another word for a job application ❑
   b) Applying for a job by 'phoning up' ❑
   c) Registering with an employment agency ❑
   d) Employers or their agents sourcing applicants by using their contacts ❑

4. How do you find out about jobs on the invisible market?
   a) By being proactive ❑
   b) By reading the right newspapers ❑
   c) By knowing your way around on the internet ❑
   d) You don't ❑

5. Which of the following is a reason why employers do not advertise positions?
   a) They find it too difficult ❑
   b) They have tried it before and it doesn't work ❑
   c) They dislike publicity ❑
   d) It puts people off ❑

6. What does 'taking control' mean?
   a) Telling employers you won't apply for their jobs unless they promise to give you an interview ❑
   b) Only applying for jobs where the salary is quoted ❑
   c) Never dealing with consultants ❑
   d) Taking responsibility for steering your job applications to successful conclusions ❑

7. In which of these situations would you most expect to find selection procedures that are formalized?
   a) In large organizations with human resources departments ❑
   b) In small, owner-run businesses ❑
   c) In the financial services sector ❑
   d) In businesses that tender for government contracts ❑

8. What is the biggest challenge you face on the visible market?
   a) Finding the time to read job ads in newspapers ❑
   b) Attending interviews ❑
   c) Engaging and overcoming competition ❑
   d) Employers who do not reply to applications ❑

9. Which of these will have most bearing on the number of applications that will be received for a job that has been advertised?
a) The salary ❏
b) The size of the advertisement ❏
c) How widely it has been advertised ❏
d) The layout and design of the advertisement ❏

10. From an applicant's point of view, what is sourcing?
a) Finding out how to write a CV ❏
b) Sending in applications ❏
c) Checking out the names of recruitment consultants ❏
d) Finding out about jobs ❏

MONDAY

You and the image you present

Teach yourself today what you have to do to acquire a winning image and, from the point of view of job applications, what a winning image is.

Starting with why it is important to consider how you come across to others, teach yourself today what steps you can take to give your image a make-over. The prize for you here is adding a value to yourself that will influence, for example, how many approaches you will receive. Your image is what others know about you and what their experience of working with you has been. If the experience has been good, then anything they have to say about you will also be good. So if a prospective employer is ringing round to do some checking up, you need have no fears. Teach yourself therefore that, if you want to acquire a winning image, it is important to give your best to every day (your lifelong interview).

Teach yourself, too, the importance of early impressions – the impressions that employers form right at the start of a selection process and that rarely leave them.

Teach yourself most of all that the image you project has to be credible so that, you, as a person, will be seen as someone who employers want:

- to engage with
- to offer a job to.

Image and why it is important

With job applications, image is usually seen in the context of going for interviews. You put on your best clothes. You make sure that your shoes are polished. You see to it that your hair is tidy and, when you get there, you put maximum effort into impressing the person sitting on the other side of the desk. Yet, this is only a small part of the story when it comes to defining the quality of the image you put across to employers and whether it is good enough. There is much more for you to consider.

The growth of the invisible market

One of the exciting phenomena of recent years is the growth of a vast and largely uncharted invisible market for jobs – one where:

- the positions are not advertised
- candidates are sourced by a variety of methods, including networking and approach.

People who know you

The rise of the invisible market underlines the vital part played by people who know you in ensuring successful outcomes to your applications. Needless to say, people who know you have a completely different view of you from the one that a complete stranger would form in the space of a 45–60-minute interview.

The lifelong interview

This brings us to the lifelong interview and the observation that, for your image to work for you today, it has not only got to be good but it has also got to be good all the time. It is no longer enough to save up your best side for interviews. With networking and approach hot on the agenda, you need to focus your attention on impressing the people you work alongside and to do this day in, day out.

Employers seek comfort

The expansion of the invisible market owes much to the reassurances that employers seek when it comes to taking on new people. In this respect, a candidate who is known to them (or who has been recommended) will stand head and shoulders above a candidate who has been sourced through a job ad (a complete stranger).

These comfort factors are at their strongest where the stakes are high (if the position to be filled is a very senior one or where it involves slotting into a small, highly integrated team). In such circumstances, no employer wants a square peg in a round hole – the disruption and cost of exiting such a person could be extreme.

What goes on behind the scenes

Even where a candidate has been sourced through an ad in the press or on a website, it is not unusual to find that

21

the employer does a little checking up before allowing the application to proceed too far. Sometimes this checking up will involve a letter or a phone call to a referee that the applicant has given – in other words, someone who can hopefully be relied on to say the right things. More potentially problematic for the applicant is the employer who decides to tap into his or her own networks for a little character background. This happens more than most people think, particularly where applicants look to move jobs within the same industry or trade (where people tend to be known to one another). Naturally, all this soliciting of information goes on behind the scenes. Applicants are kept in the dark – they rarely find out if the pitch has been queered for them by someone they know.

> Do not expect anyone to put in a good word for you if they know your character and/or work record are flawed. Remember that their own reputation is put on the line with any recommendations they make. They will not stick their neck out unless they feel it is safe.

Give your image a make-over

Taking on board the lifelong interview and its importance in today's world of jobs, can you honestly say you give your best to every day? If the answer is no, then this is where you start. Do not forget that your image is at stake and, as we have seen, this plays a crucial part in any success you will have when it comes to applying for jobs.

Your performance

Needless to say, the standard of your work has much to do with how others view you. If you are good at your job, this will go a long way towards creating a successful image.

Where some high performers fall down, however, is by failing to give 100 per cent all of the time. The message? Do not have off days. If you do, it will earn you the reputation of being someone whose commitment is up and down. This will serve to put a dent in the image that you are trying to create.

How you get on with others

The ability to work in or manage teams is such a major issue in selection that how you handle your relationships with others will always be an item for scrutiny. You must be mindful that your lifelong interview has a 360° orientation.

Bosses, peers and subordinates all hold opinions about you and the fact that you are good to work with has got to come across to everyone. Two particular points to bear in mind are:

● Don't blame others when it is your fault.
● Don't run down your colleagues behind their backs (keep your opinions about people to yourself).

Your character

Everyone has flaws, but the trick is not to advertise them and this is not always easy with people you are in contact with daily. In practice it means:

● not getting too close to colleagues (learning to be friendly without being familiar)

23

- keeping a firm control on any messages you send out about yourself
- being careful what you say about yourself on social networking sites.

Your appearance

Your image has much to do with your appearance and, while most people understand about looking smart when they go for interviews, they pay far less attention to the impact they make every day.

Turning over a new leaf

Finally, with regard to giving your image a face-lift, remember that it is never too late to turn over a new leaf. You may feel that you have blotted your copy book irretrievably and, yes, the old skeletons can still come rattling out of the cupboard to haunt you (that is all part of the lifelong interview). However, as the grey areas in your track record recede further and further into the past, they pale increasingly into insignificance.

Early impressions

At the start of most job applications, you will be a complete unknown to the employer. Therefore, whether you get the job or not will depend on how you come across:

● in your CV, letter of application, etc.
● at any interviews you attend.

The halo effect

Professional interviewers are trained to be aware of the halo effect. The halo effect is the tendency to see some good points in a candidate early on in the selection process and, from there on, to ignore any flaws that come to light. The halo effect can also work in reverse – bad points can register at the beginning and cloud more favourable impressions that surface later on. Non-professional interviewers are most susceptible to halo effects, for example, line managers.

Early impressions stick

The halo effect teaches us:

● the importance of early impressions
● how early impressions stick.

From your point of view, this means paying special attention to the image you project in the opening stages of any job application and in particular:

- the quality and presentation of your CV, letter of application and any forms you fill in
- the way you handle any telephone calls from prospective employers (e.g. telephone calls to arrange interviews)
- the first few minutes of any interview.

What you put across in these opening stages will tend to set the agenda for what follows. You send out an impression and, good or bad, that impression will be very difficult to shift.

Credibility

Are you as good as your CV makes you out to be? An employer will need some convincing, and crucial to this process is ensuring that you do not do anything that will give them reason to doubt you.

The importance of consistency

Inconsistencies are top of the list of ways in which candidates can damage their credibility. An example of an inconsistency is the candidate who gives pay as the reason for leaving a job on an application form and then says something entirely different at an interview. It may seem trivial, but to an employer who doesn't know you from Adam or Eve, such inconsistencies will cast doubts over your whole application.

The message? Make sure that any information you give to an employer marries with information you have given elsewhere – otherwise your image (credibility) will suffer. In particular, be careful about matching any information contained in:

- your CV
- letters of application
- online applications
- application forms
- forms you fill in for head-hunters or consultants
- statements you make at interviews.

Some employers will query minor slips. Others will not. They will simply write you off as untrustworthy and your application will fail for this reason alone.

> **TIP**
>
> *To ensure that you do not fall into the trap of contradicting yourself, always keep copies of any documentation that you submit to an employer so that you can:*
>
> - *check that the information you give in each is consistent*
> - *read through what you have said about yourself before you go for an interview.*

Engagement factors

Why is it that employers are drawn to some candidates and not to others? In terms of image, what makes the difference?

Successful candidates tend to be those who are good at projecting themselves as they really are. Employers find they have something to latch on to (a real person they can warm to) and the engagement factors start to work. This contrasts with the candidate who tries to put on a false image and ends up coming across as a cardboard cut-out. Employers will feel either that they have not connected with the real person or, worse still, that something is being hidden from them.

The power of you

In any competitive employment situation, what marks you out from the rest of humanity (your individuality, style, uniqueness) is important and you should focus on using it in the following ways:

- Your CV: thinking that they are doing the right thing, many candidates have their CVs professionally prepared or they use some standard format they have found in a book or downloaded off a website. The result is a CV that reads like everyone else's – this will not necessarily do you any favours when trying to reach out to employers who are bombarded with applications. Have a go at doing your own CV. Use words and phrases that are familiar to you. Let those little bits of you come out.
- Interview techniques: do not get hung up about rehearsing fancy interview techniques. Try to be natural instead. It is the real you that people will engage with. It is the real you that you need them to see.
- Your appearance: in your choice of clothes and accessories for an interview, avoid being seen as just another 'suit'. Preferably (and without being outlandish) put on something that makes a statement about you and your tastes, for instance a tie that you particularly like or a favourite piece of jewellery. Note also that interviewers often bring candidates back to mind by reference to something they wore at the interview. (This is covered in more detail on Thursday.)

Summary

Today you have taught yourself:

- the importance of image
- the importance of having the right one.

Because of the risks of taking on a misfit or a potential litigant, more and more employers today resort to tapping in to their networks to find out what they can about people who apply for jobs. They are less inclined to take individuals on trust because they know how difficult it can be to exit people who come in and start causing trouble. You have taught yourself today that, in the business of bringing job applications to successful conclusions, a favourable image counts for far more than anything else. So forget the smart answers to tough questions and focus instead on your lifelong interview – the image you project to others every day and how you can improve it.

Finally, today you have taught yourself to recognize the power of you as an individual because, at the end of the day, your individuality is what makes you attractive to employers. You have also taught yourself today how you can bring 'that little bit of you' into your job applications and then take the image you have projected forward to the point where the employer is happy to offer you the job.

SUNDAY
MONDAY
TUESDAY
WEDNESDAY
THURSDAY
FRIDAY
SATURDAY

Fact-check (answers at the back)

1. What is your lifelong interview?
   a) The image you project to people you work with every day ❑
   b) An interview for a job you have been for before ❑
   c) A learning programme ❑
   d) What your bosses have said about you at appraisal interviews ❑

2. What are comfort factors?
   a) Factors that determine how easy it will be to get on with you ❑
   b) A matrix used at interviews for measuring performance ❑
   c) The reassurances employers like to have before they make job offers ❑
   d) Factors for determining who goes on the interview list ❑

3) How do you go about improving your image?
   a) Buy a better car ❑
   b) Work on your lifelong interview ❑
   c) Take elocution lessons ❑
   d) Dump your partner ❑

4. What is the halo effect?
   a) The tendency to look for a candidate's good points ❑
   b) The effect you can create at an interview by arriving smartly dressed ❑
   c) The tendency to see good points in a candidate in the early stages of a selection process and thereafter to ignore any flaws ❑
   d) The effect when one candidate for a job is streets ahead of the others ❑

5. What are engagement factors?
   a) The same as comfort factors ❑
   b) Factors that draw employers to candidates ❑
   c) Matches between the employer's specification and what you have to offer ❑
   d) Terms for negotiation in the final stages leading up to an offer of employment ❑

6. Which of the following will have most impact on your chances of landing a top job?
   a) A new set of clothes straight off the catwalk ❑
   b) Interview coaching from a top expert ❑
   c) Your vision of the future ❑
   d) Good reports from people who have worked with you ❑

7. When you are applying for a job, what is the best way of making sure you keep your credibility intact?
   a) By not telling lies ❑
   b) By making sure everything you say about yourself is consistent ❑
   c) By only giving the names of referees who can be relied on to say something good about you ❑
   d) By keeping your answers to questions at interviews short ❑

8. When it comes to preparing a CV, who is the best person to do the job?
a) You ☐
b) A professional CV writer ☐
c) An outplacement counsellor ☐
d) One of your friends who has worked in human resources ☐

9. What is the best tip for presenting yourself to an interviewer?
a) Wear a fashionable outfit ☐
b) Try hard to hide your accent ☐
c) Be yourself ☐
d) Before you go, take a course in interview techniques ☐

10. Given the need to look smart, what clothes should you choose for an interview?
a) Clothes that say something about you and your tastes ☐
b) Clothes that are not too stylish ☐
c) Dark-coloured clothes ☐
d) Clothes that make you look older ☐

TUESDAY

Selection
criteria

Teach yourself today how to get into employers' thinking. What are they looking for in candidates for their jobs (their selection criteria) and what do you have that will make them see you as someone who answers their needs?

Teach yourself today to spot clues because it is from these clues that you can put together pictures that will tell you whether it is worth giving jobs a shot or not. However – and more importantly – teach yourself today to focus on the matches between what employers want and what you have to offer because these will be the strong areas of your applications – areas that you will be doing your best to bring into prominence as the selection process moves forward. Equally, teach yourself today to identify any weak areas because it is just as important to know where the problems could be coming from. Perhaps most important of all today, teach yourself to condition your expectations when you go out onto the job market. You won't get an interview every time you apply for a job and you could be on the market for a long time. Teach yourself today therefore what it takes to keep going and deal with the disappointments that are bound to come up from time to time.

What employers look for

At the outset of every job application, one of the first questions you should ask yourself is 'What are my chances of success?' or, more precisely, 'What is this particular employer looking for and is it me?'

Clues in advertisements

Let's begin with the first part of this question – how do you tell what qualities employers look for in candidates? What clues do you have to their thinking?

If you have sourced the job on the visible market (i.e. through an advertisement in the press or on a website), then a few clues to the employer's selection criteria can usually be found in the ad itself. Obvious criteria, such as 'applicants must be fluent in at least two European languages', are there for everyone to see but, by reading ads carefully, you can often pick up some interesting insights into:

● the way that employers' minds work
● how employers will view any candidates who apply.

> ## Example
>
> An ad for an engineer we saw recently talked at great length about the company's extensive overseas customer base. You can read into this that applications from stay-at-home Joes and Janes probably will not be too well received. Furthermore, people with few or no domestic ties are more likely to get preference.

Read ads carefully and keep your eyes peeled for the coded text.

Hidden criteria

How employers see themselves and the jobs they have to offer is often based on their judgements as to 'what works here' and 'who fits in and who doesn't'. For instance, 'Life's a pig in this organization – anyone with any kind of home life will soon get fed up' means that candidates with young families or outside interests should exit at this point. Call them prejudices if you like, but many of these hidden criteria relate to bad experiences that employers have had. Time and money has been spent on training someone who left after a few months, and a mental note has been made never to recruit anyone like that again. You have no control over hidden criteria. In most cases, you will not even know they exist and only an oddball question at an interview will warn you of their presence.

Note: well-qualified candidates, baffled at why they did not get the job, often need look no further than one of these hidden criteria.

Tapping into your networks

One important and often overlooked way to pick up some clues on how employers view people is by tapping into your networks. Do you know anyone who has inside information on the employer with the job that interests you? If so, give your contact a ring and see what you can find out.

People who have made applications previously can also be very useful sources of information on what employers view as important. Therefore, include in your ring round any people you know who are (or have recently been) active on the job market.

If you sourced the job by networking, your contact is an obvious place to start when it comes to getting some information.

Picking consultants' brains

We saw on Sunday how a large part of the invisible job market was accessed through consultants of various types, notably:

● recruitment consultants (agencies)
● search consultants or head-hunters.

Consultants are usually storehouses of information on employers' likes and dislikes and, because it is their business to know, they should be able to provide you with all sorts of information on the criteria that will be used to assess you.

No placement, no fee

In most cases, a consultant will have a vested interest in you getting the job, because all or a sizeable chunk of their fee will only be payable if and when you start.

Inspired guesswork

Do not hesitate to put two and two together and make a few inspired guesses at what employers see as desirable attributes in candidates. For example, it is a reasonable guess that a paternalistic employer would feel more at home with a candidate who has stayed in jobs for long periods of time, whereas a 'flat' organization may look more favourably on someone who has moved around (someone who will not get too wound up about the lack of promotion prospects).

All employers are different

There are no cast-iron rules when it comes to selection criteria. They vary from one employer to the next and that is how they should be viewed. It is a mistake to think that all employers see things the same way. They do not.

Pick out your strong and weak areas

You should now have a list of selection criteria for the job you have set your sights on and your list should include:

- any experience and/or qualifications that would be seen as particularly desirable
- a type of training or attainment of a certain level of competence that would be a plus point
- knowledge of a particular technique or method that would be advantageous
- any personal attribute that would be a factor in selection (e.g. appearance, personality, etc.)
- superlatives that are called for, i.e. exceptional ability over and above the norm
- any kind of background that would be preferred (e.g. someone who has lived overseas may be seen as more suitable for an ex-patriate post)

● any unusual selection criteria, such as the ability to put in long hours at short notice or the capacity and infrastructure to work from home.

With your list you can now move on to the next step – comparing yourself with the criteria and seeing if you match up.

The ideal candidate

Let's start by dispelling a myth. There is no such thing as the ideal candidate. This is said here to stop you from only seeing your shortcomings and from immediately jumping to the conclusion that you do not stand any chance of getting the job.

Anyone who has worked in selection will tell you that candidates for a job are usually a wide mix. True, there are always a few people who automatically go on the turn-down pile, but the rest (the vast majority) are made up of individuals who qualify for the job in different ways. Candidate A's academic achievements are spot on; Candidate B has some very interesting experience; Candidate C, however, is located in exactly the right place, and so on. No one candidate has all the attributes, yet some come pretty close, and this is the basis on which interview lists are decided.

Strong areas

Let's focus for a moment on what is good about your
application. These are your strong areas – in other words,
where there is a match between:

● what you have to offer
● what the employer is looking for.

A strong area could, for example, be that you are very familiar
with the software package that the employer mentioned in
the advertisement. Alternatively, it could be the fact that you
are used to unsociable hours and the job occasionally involves
working nights.

> Your strong areas are your most effective weapons
> when it comes to engaging and overcoming competition.
> Get ready to use them.

Weak areas

It is equally important to identify the weak areas in your
application – areas where you do not have the attributes that
the employer seeks or where what you have to offer falls short
in some significant way.

> With weak areas the big mistake is to ignore them because
> you would prefer to forget that they are there. Weak areas
> need dealing with and first you have to face up to them
> and assess the threat they pose.

It could be, for instance, that you have all the right experience,
qualifications and so forth for a job, but on the grapevine you
hear that the company's management team are all in their 30s,
whereas you are 49. Because it would be discriminatory they
are unlikely to turn you down because you are too old, hence
we are dealing (potentially) with a hidden selection criteria.
How to proceed?

● Identify the weak area – the area of potential disadvantage.
● Start to think of ways to overcome it.

Pre-emptive strikes

In the example above, treat the knowledge you have of the age structure of the company's management team as privileged information and see how it can be put to use. Could you, for example, introduce into your application that you are used to working with colleagues across a wide range of age groups? Could you thereby reduce their fears that you are a potential misfit? Could it get you a place on the interview list?

Are you wasting your time?

With job applications, whether you are wasting your time is a judgement you have to make if you find that your skills, qualifications and experience do not seem to match what the employer is seeking. Do you give it a whirl or are you wasting your time?

Providing you stay detached and tell yourself not to get too upset about the turn-downs, there is no harm at all in applying for jobs that look good but where you do not quite meet all the stipulations. Sometimes employers assemble such formidable lists of 'essential' skills, qualifications and other attributes that they end up with:

● few applicants (those who were not put off)
● no one with all the attributes
● many near misses instead.

This is where you could get your chance.

Rating your chances of success

Having gone through the exercise of picking out the strong and weak areas in your application, it should be possible for you to make an assessment of your chances of success. If you have lots of strong areas, you should be in for a fairly smooth ride. If, however, there are some glaring weaknesses in your application, you need to be prepared to pull out the stops. For instance, you may need to turn your mind to effecting a few pre-emptive strikes.

Expectations

This is a gentle warning. Rating your chances of success is one thing, whereas building up your expectations is another. The modern job market is an unpredictable place where practically anything can happen.

Example

A young woman applicant received a turn-down letter for a job for which she was abundantly well qualified. The reason? The employer decided to put its recruiting plans on hold. They did not think to explain this in their letter to her and she was left wondering where she had gone wrong.

Discouragement

Discouragement is what happens when your job applications keep going nowhere – when your doormat is littered with 'Sorry, but no thank you,' letters. You feel you are banging your head against a brick wall and, sooner or later, despair starts to set in. Finally, you stop applying for jobs because you feel you cannot take any more.

We are all human and discouragement can and does get to us. Here is a five-point plan for dealing with it:

1 Stop (take a holiday from your job applications).
2 Take stock of what you are doing and try to see where you might be going wrong.
3 Do not be surprised if you cannot find anything that you are doing wrong.
4 Remind yourself that success on the job market means being prepared to take the hard knocks.
5 Do not start again until you are fully recovered, otherwise the feeling of discouragement will soon be back again.

Summary

SUNDAY
MONDAY
TUESDAY
WEDNESDAY
THURSDAY
FRIDAY
SATURDAY

You have taught yourself today to look at every job you source and, before you do anything, to see what matches you can find between:

- what the employer wants
- what you have to offer.

From these matches (or the lack of them) you have taught yourself today how to form a view of:

- whether or not it is worth applying for the job
- if you do apply, what it is about you that the employer will find most interesting.

From this piece of analysis, you have taught yourself today the importance of identifying the strong and weak areas of your application. Strong areas are what you will be seeking to focus attention on as the selection process moves forward. Weak areas are where the awkward questions will come from – questions for which you will need to have answers or where you may have to have a pre-emptive strike up your sleeve.

Finally, you have taught yourself today that the job market will not always be nice or fair to you. Sometimes you will have to shrug off disappointment. Sometimes, you will have to pick yourself off the floor so you are fit and ready to start all over again.

Fact-check (answers at the back)

1. What are selection criteria?
   a) How employers score candidates they interview ❏
   b) What employers see as the key requirements for a job ❏
   c) What candidates see as their key attributes ❏
   d) The list of questions that will be put to candidates when they are interviewed ❏

2. What are hidden criteria?
   a) Criteria that do not matter ❏
   b) Criteria for jobs on the invisible market ❏
   c) Criteria for top jobs ❏
   d) The criteria that candidates never know about ❏

3. What is 'no placement, no fee'?
   a) Where recruitment consultants offer a free service ❏
   b) When recruitment consultants do not charge a fee until someone starts work ❏
   c) Where recruitment consultants waive their fee in return for other business ❏
   d) Where recruitment consultants' fees are not dependent on someone starting ❏

4. Which of these statements is correct?
   a) Most candidates are unsuitable ❏
   b) Most candidates are suitable ❏
   c) Most candidates are suitable in different ways ❏
   d) Most candidates are 'don't knows' ❏

5. What is a 'pre-emptive strike'?
   a) A way of introducing information at an interview that will serve to head off a negative view of you being formed ❏
   b) A way of leading an interviewer away from an awkward line of questioning ❏
   c) A way of asserting yourself over an interviewer ❏
   d) A way of engaging in an argument with an interviewer without causing offence ❏

6. What is it best to do when you start to feel discouraged by your lack of success?
   a) Stop and take stock ❏
   b) Ignore the feeling of discouragement and carry on ❏
   c) Do a course in building confidence ❏
   d) Give up ❏

7. What do you do when you do not have all the qualifications for a job?
   a) Give it a whirl ❏
   b) As **a**, but do not be surprised if you get turned down, i.e. condition your expectations ❏
   c) Give it a miss ❏
   d) Phone up first, explain where your qualifications fall short and ask if it is worth applying ❏

8. What is the best way of ensuring that your job applications are successful?

a) Spend money on a good CV ☐

b) Learn about interview techniques ☐

c) Apply for as many jobs as possible ☐

d) Apply for jobs where there are matches between what employers want and what you have to offer ☐

9. When it comes to finding out about employers' likes and dislikes why will you find recruitment consultants keen to help you?

a) It is part of their job ☐

b) They are trained to be helpful ☐

c) Most of them are paid on commission so it is in their interests to see you get the job ☐

d) Their phone calls are monitored. They could be in trouble for not being helpful ☐

10. Is it worth applying for a job where you don't have too many matches?

a) No ☐

b) Yes ☐

c) Yes, providing you keep your expectations in check ☐

d) Yes, providing you have got nothing better to do at the time ☐

WEDNESDAY

Getting interviews

Teach yourself today how to get interviews, which is the first challenge you face when you apply for jobs.

Teach yourself today how employers pick interview lists and how you can use this knowledge of what goes on behind the scenes to your advantage. Teach yourself today that getting interviews will be harder when there are many more applicants for the job. Teach yourself that in these situations employers are very choosy about who they invite in and why your application has got to hit them first time (it won't get another chance!).

Teach yourself today what it takes to grab employers' attention and what treatment you need to give to:

- your CV
- any letters of application you write
- any application forms you are asked to fill in.

Teach yourself today the importance of your availability, which means:

- making it easy for employers to contact you
- being there to take their calls.

Teach yourself today how to carry out an availability audit to see how employer friendly you really are. Teach yourself how to learn from an availability audit and what steps to take when you find you could be unintentionally putting obstacles in the path of employers who are trying to get hold of you.

The challenge you face

Interviews are very time-consuming. Depending on the seniority of the job and the interviewer's style, an interview can last on average between 45 and 90 minutes. Small wonder, therefore, that employers are very choosy about who they ask along. Irrespective of how well qualified you are for a job, you should never take it for granted that you are going to get an interview. The fact that you are the best thing since sliced bread is not enough. That message has to get through to the employer and the responsibility to make sure that this happens falls on you (yet another example of 'taking control').

Competition

The challenge is of course most in evidence where there is competition for the job. For example:

- where the employer has a number of applicants to choose from
- where some applicants will be picked out for interview and some will not.

The challenge of getting on interview lists is one you particularly need to focus your mind on when making applications on the visible market. Any good job that has been advertised (in newspapers, journals or on websites) will attract large numbers of applicants and you should always allow for this.

How interview lists are chosen

Yesterday we looked at selection criteria – the benchmarks that employers use to assess candidates. We saw how selection criteria provide you with a basis to determine the strong and weak areas in your application:

- A strong area: where there is a match between the selection criteria and what you have to offer.
- A weak area: where you fall short of the criteria in some way.

Similarly, an employer browsing through a batch of job applications will be searching for matches. If a sufficient number of matches with the selection criteria are found, the candidate will be put on the 'Yes' pile. Alternatively, if few or no matches are evident, the candidate will be put on the pile to be turned down. Other points to note about this preliminary sifting process are:

- Where there are large numbers of applications, the time given to reading each one will be relatively short.
- Not all applications will be read from start to finish.
- Applications are rarely read twice (once on the turn-down pile, they tend to stay there).

Improve your chances of being picked for interviews by helping employers to make the matches. Take control of your applications and give your strong areas prominence. In doing this, pay special attention to any documentation that you submit to employers, notably:

- *your CV*
- *your letters of application*
- *any forms you are asked to fill in.*

Reviewing and customizing your CV

One of the prime functions of a CV is to get you interviews. It will not, however, perform this function effectively if you use the same standard CV for every application. A CV needs to be reviewed and customized every time you use it. Design your CV for the job you want it to do.

Customizing your CV means:

- looking at the job you are applying for and considering the selection criteria
- seeing to what extent the criteria are reflected in your qualifications, work history, experience, etc.
- bringing the matches into prominence by affording them greater space and summarizing them in your key achievements
- conversely, relegating or omitting information that has little or no relevance to the job.

Example

Simon C is applying for a job with a firm that employs fewer than 50 people. So Simon redesigns his CV to bring into prominence his experience in managing small teams. He makes rather less mention of the time he spent working on projects for a large multinational company.

Get your strong areas mentioned at the start

As mentioned earlier, applications and supporting information, such as CVs, do not always get read from start to finish. There is a switch-off point part-way through – a candidate can get dumped simply because they left the best bits until last. In your CV, ensure that the strong areas in your application are mentioned early on. A summary of your key achievements on the first page is one way of doing this.

As any fiction writer will tell you, the best way to grab a reader's attention is with a good juicy bit at the beginning.

Putting together a letter of application

When you mail a CV to an employer, you usually put a covering letter with it. This is another opportunity to list the strong areas of your application. Do not worry about repeating information that you have already given in your CV.

What to include in your letter of application:

● Make it clear which job you are applying for by referring to the job title (the one used in the ad) and to the newspaper in which it appeared. Quote a reference if one was given.
● Set out how you feel you meet the criteria for the job, i.e. your strong areas. A short list of bullet points will suffice here.

- Tell the employer how to get hold of you (phone numbers, when it's best to contact you, etc. – more on this in the section 'Be there to take the calls' below).
- Keep your letter short and to the point.
- Remember to sign the letter – failing to do so gives the impression that it is one of a batch you sent out and this will hardly endear you to a prospective employer.

Application forms

You may or may not be asked to complete an application form prior to being invited for an interview. Some employers may be happy to see you on the basis of your CV. Others may prefer to know a little more about you before they commit themselves.

Application forms and CVs

Candidates sometimes feel confused when they send a copy of their CV to an employer and then they are asked to fill in an application form. The application form, they are quick to notice, asks for more or less the same information all over again. So what do they conclude?

- Either no one took the trouble to read their CV (hours of toil went into its preparation)
- Or the form is just another piece of paper – unimportant and peripheral to their chances of getting the job.

The knock-on effect, all too often, is one of the following:

- The candidate goes off in a huff and the form is not returned.
- The form is returned with 'see my CV' written in some or all of the spaces.
- The form is dashed off in ten minutes, complete with crossings out, spelling mistakes, untidy writing and questions that fall into the 'too hard' category left unanswered.

This is a pity because being sent an application form is probably a sign that the candidate's CV has found favour and that an interview is in the offing. However, by failing to send the form back or by sending it back in a half-completed or scruffy state, the effort that went into preparing the CV is now entirely wasted. The moral? It may take a great CV to get you noticed in today's tough job markets, but a great CV does not do much good unless you can follow it up with an equally impressive application form. It is rather like baking a beautiful cake. It takes all the ingredients to make it turn out just right.

Give proper importance to application forms

In the business of moving you from A to B and then on to C in any selection process, an important aspect is to deal properly with any application forms put in front of you. This means:

- treating every application form you fill in as a fresh challenge and never seeing any form as 'like the rest' or as a simple exercise in taking extracts from your CV
- appreciating that employers have widely varying needs and concerns – never see any of their questions as unnecessary or intrusive

- appreciating that employers will have good reasons for asking you to fill in a form.

Example

'To pick an interview list we need to compare candidates like-for-like and, particularly where there are a large number of candidates for a job, this is not very easy to do by scanning a batch of CVs for the simple reason they don't conform to any standard pattern. What we find we have to do is cast our eyes here, there and everywhere for the information we're seeking whereas with our standard application form this problem doesn't arise. With every candidate the information is in the same place.'

Quote from a human resources manager in the engineering industry

Mention your strong areas

One of the difficulties with application forms is that, with their question and answer format, they do not seem to give you much latitude for telling the story as you want it told. How do you proceed?

On many application forms there is a big blank space that stares at you, usually somewhere towards the end. The space invites you to give any further information you consider relevant to your application (or similar wording), leaving you to ponder on what information the employer could possibly have in mind. You have already listed all your personal information, your qualifications and your job experience, so what else is it they want to know?

54

Partly because they feel they should say something, many candidates end up filling these spaces with statements about themselves that add little or nothing to their chances of getting the job. At best, they repeat information they have given elsewhere on the form. At worst, they go into self-eulogies that have the opposite effect on employers to the one intended. By inserting these spaces on their forms, employers are really saying to you 'OK, we've put all the questions so far, but now it's your turn to tell us why we should be viewing your application seriously.'

Application forms are read

Unlike CVs and other documentation that candidates submit at the early stages of making an application, application forms are actually read by employers, and often very carefully. Use these 'further information' spaces on forms, therefore, to list your strong areas: 'I feel I am well qualified to do this job because...' and give your reasons in the form of bullet points.

What if the form does not have a space for further information? Staple an additional sheet of paper to the form and use that instead.

A useful tip with application forms is to photocopy them first. Use the photocopy to do a draft. In this way, you avoid blobs of correcting fluid and squeezed up writing on the finished version. Neither will do you much good on the first impressions front.

Keep a copy of everything you send to an employer, including your completed application form. The reason for this was explained on Monday. You will need to revisit the application form, along with any documents you have submitted, prior to going for an interview. Only by keeping a copy will you be able to ensure that anything you say is consistent with what you have put in writing.

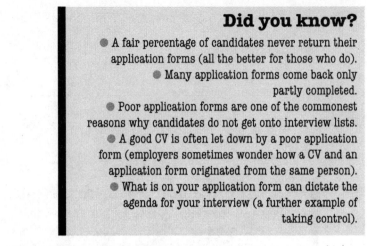

Did you know?

● A fair percentage of candidates never return their application forms (all the better for those who do).

● Many application forms come back only partly completed.

● Poor application forms are one of the commonest reasons why candidates do not get onto interview lists.

● A good CV is often let down by a poor application form (employers sometimes wonder how a CV and an application form originated from the same person).

● What is on your application form can dictate the agenda for your interview (a further example of taking control).

Be there to take the calls

Most interviews are fixed up over the telephone and so an important part of getting you to interviews is to make sure that you are there to take the calls.

How interviews are arranged

● Employers tend to move quickly when it comes to setting up interviews.

- They use the phone to make contact with the candidates they want to see.
- The calls can come at any time – evenings are particularly good for catching people at home (where they will be away from office eavesdroppers and able to speak more freely).
- Employers do not waste time on people they find hard to contact – especially when there are plenty of other candidates to choose from.
- Telephone availability plays a big part in determining whether you get on the interview list or not.

Consultants

Consultants are another reason why more and more contact with candidates is by phone. Consultants of one form or another are involved in an ever-increasing number of recruitment exercises. Consultants are habitual users of the phone and they rarely communicate by any other means.

> 'Why didn't I get picked for an interview?' is the question that every unsuccessful candidate asks. 'Why didn't they ask to see me when I've got all the qualifications for the job?'
>
> The answer in many cases is a very simple one: these are the people who were not there to take the calls. Of course, the rejection letter they received did not tell them that.

'Employer friendly'

'Employer friendly' means making employers' lives as easy as possible and not placing any barriers in their paths. It is also another aspect of taking control: smoothing the course along which you want your application to go.

Your CV

As part of employer friendliness, most people are aware of the need to include telephone points of contact in their CV.

'Points of contact' means:

- your home phone number
- the number you can be contacted on at work
- the number of your mobile.

Let's look at each of these in turn.

Your home telephone number

Phoning candidates in the evening, when they get home from work, is favoured by many recruiters because it provides the facility to talk freely. Therefore, ways to make yourself more employer friendly include:

- giving a rough idea of the time you normally arrive home in your CV, for example, 'after 6.30 p.m.' inserted alongside your home phone number
- considering any routine ins and outs, for instance, if you are routinely out on Tuesdays and Thursdays because you play squash and attend an evening class, make sure to mention this.

Work numbers

Consider whether your name would be instantly recognized by whoever answers the phone at work. If not, it may be a good idea to insert an extension number in your CV or the name of the department where you are based.

Mobile phones

On the face of it, mobile phones provide the perfect answer to telephone availability. Any snags? Only if your mobile is switched off for long periods because of your job or if you are regularly in areas where signal strength is poor. The answer is to make sure that you check your voicemail messages and missed calls regularly. People who do not return their messages are a recruiter's nightmare. Moreover, if you return a call late, you may find that the interviews have already been arranged.

> By giving a choice of home, work and mobile phone numbers, you are giving employers more than one way of contacting you. This is important where people, such as managers and consultants, work to tight timescales and where the need to get you in for an interview is urgent.

Your letter of application

Restating your telephone points of contact in your letter of application does no harm at all. This is all part of employer friendliness and keeps a controlling hand on the path of your application.

Test your home telephone availability

Here is an interesting exercise for you to try. Put yourself in the position of someone trying to get hold of you. You have given your home phone number in your CV. You said you are normally in after 6.30 p.m. Now put this to the test over, say, a two-week period. Employers on the whole will take you literally. They will phone you at 6.30 p.m. and, if they fail to get through for any reason, they may try again ten minutes later. Monitor what would happen if someone tried ringing you at 6.30 p.m. and 6.40 p.m. on the dot each evening Monday to Friday.

- Would you be in?
- Would anyone be in?
- Most importantly, how many times would the number ring out engaged?

The aim of this exercise is to expose flaws in your availability – flaws that will probably surprise you, for instance:

- the number of times you are late
- the number of times you pick up the phone the minute you walk through the door
- how often other people in the family are on the phone or using the line to access the internet.

An availability audit such as this is intended to throw up points for action. Included on the list could be:

- Is 6.30 p.m. a little ambitious? Would saying 7.00 p.m. would be better (just to be on the safe side)?
- Do you need to introduce some disciplines at home during periods when you are applying for jobs (e.g. no blocking the line between 6.30 p.m. and 7.30 p.m. in the evenings)?
- Do you need a call minder facility, possibly with a link to your mobile phone, so you are alerted if someone is trying to get through?

Summary

Today you have taught yourself to view getting an interview as a challenge and, in the case of jobs for which there will be a large number of applicants, the toughest challenge of all. Somehow you have got to catch the eye of someone who:

- does not know you
- only has the information you have put on your application to go on.

Today you have taught yourself how to:

- design a CV that will bring the strong areas of your application into prominence
- write letters of application that will do the same
- fill in application forms in the way that employers want.

You have taught yourself that controlling messages to employers in this way gives you the best chance of being picked for an interview.

Lastly, today you have taught yourself the importance of your availability. When employers phone, you will be there to take the calls. Your application will not therefore end up on the pile put to one side because no one answered or the voicemail message was not returned. On the contrary, everything about you so far has been 'employer friendly' and, in a world which has no time for people who come across as 'difficult', this will count heavily in your favour.

SUNDAY
MONDAY
TUESDAY
WEDNESDAY
THURSDAY
FRIDAY
SATURDAY

Fact-check (answers at the back)

1. What is a strong area?
   a) An area where you have most experience ❑
   b) An area where there is a match between what the employer wants and what you have to offer ❑
   c) An area that is not a weak area ❑
   d) The subject you can talk about best ❑

2. In what situation is it most important to get your strong areas across?
   a) When you are talking to a head-hunter ❑
   b) When you are being interviewed by a novice ❑
   c) When you need a job in a hurry ❑
   d) When there are a lot of other applicants for the job ❑

3. In the CV you submit, where is best to mention your strong areas?
   a) At the beginning ❑
   b) In the middle ❑
   c) At the end ❑
   d) Don't – mention them in the supporting letter you send in ❑

4. What should you do when you are asked to fill in an application form and the information requested is the same as the information that you have already provided in your CV?

   a) Write 'see CV' on the application form and return it ❑
   b) As **a**, but staple another CV to the application form ❑
   c) Ignore the application form (don't send it back) ❑
   d) Fill it in, i.e. repeat the information you have already given ❑

5. What stands most chance of being read?
   a) CV ❑
   b) Application form ❑
   c) Letter written in support of an application ❑
   d) All of the above stand an equal chance. ❑

6. What is the main reason why candidates miss out on interviews?
   a) Their CV is not good enough ❑
   b) Their CV is too long ❑
   c) They could not get time off work to go to the interview ❑
   d) They could not be contacted ❑

7. What is an availability audit?
   a) A way of testing how easy it is for employers to contact you ❑
   b) Asking a friend to look at your CV ❑
   c) Making sure that you have given your strong areas prominence ❑

d) A method of reviewing the progress of a job application ❏

8. Why is it important to keep a copy of everything you send to employers?
a) In case you have to chase them up ❏
b) In case they lose their papers ❏
c) So you can remind yourself what you said before you go in for an interview ❏
d) In case you get turned down ❏

9. What action do you take when you are told that you have not been selected for an interview?
a) Phone up the employer and tell them they have got it wrong ❏
b) Make a note not to apply to the same employer again ❏
c) Phone up the employer and ask them to give you reasons for their decision ❏
d) None ❏

10. Which of the following is a way of guaranteeing that your name gets on the interview list?
a) Phone up at the start and say that you won't apply for the job unless you are guaranteed an interview ❏
b) Go to the employer's offices and demand that someone sees you ❏
c) Make a few false claims in your CV ❏
d) There is no way. ❏

THUURSDAY

Going for interviews

Teach yourself today all you need to know about preparing for interviews and what you need to consider before you go. Teach yourself that there are different types of interview and that no one size fits all when it comes to deciding the best approach to use. Teach yourself, too, that interviewers are not all the same either. Some will be slick professionals, but others will be hard-pressed managers who are not used to interviewing and may have little idea what they are doing. Teach yourself to be aware of these differences in interviews and interviewers and how to allow for them.

Teach yourself today how to be ready for the questions you are likely to be asked at interviews and how to answer them. Teach yourself the importance of keeping your answers to questions concise and, in this way, help to make sure that your interviews don't flop because they run out of time.

Teach yourself today what to take to interviews and why it is important before you go to revisit any information you have already given to the employer (e.g. the information in your CV). Teach yourself also how to do some research on the employer so you know what to say if the interviewer asks without warning 'What do you know about us?' Teach yourself today how to answer questions like these.

Types of interview

What kind of interview can you expect? What kinds of question will you be asked and how will the person sitting on the other side of the desk form an opinion about you?

No two interviews are the same, but you can predict the pattern they follow by putting them into categories. These categories are determined by:

- how you sourced the job (e.g. did you see the job advertised or was it an opportunity you got to hear about through one of your contacts?)
- who is doing the interview.

Preliminary interviews

Where there are a lot of applicants for a job, employers will probably feel the need to carry out preliminary interviews.

These preliminary interviews will be designed to:

- sort the wheat from the chaff
- reduce the applicants to a more manageable number for final selection purposes.

Key points to note about preliminary interviews are:

- The interviewer will seek to establish 'broad suitability', rather than decide who to offer the job to.
- Candidates are often seen in a procession one after the other. Therefore, time is a factor. Interviewers will be keen not to overrun because of the knock-on effect this will have on interviews later in the day.
- Preliminary interviews are hard work. Even the most seasoned interviewers can start to flag and go into robotic mode after doing a string of them.

Short-list interviews

Once the preliminary interviews have been held, some of the candidates will be asked to come back for a second or short-list interview.

Note

The challenge you face when you get to the short-list is looked at on Saturday.

Interviews for jobs sourced proactively

The invitation to go for an interview could be generated by one of the following events:

● Your unsolicited CV lands on the right desk at the right time.
● An introduction is made through a firm of consultants.
● You have tapped into your contacts (networking).

Interviews for jobs sourced proactively are very different, notably:

● You may be the only candidate (or one of a very small number).
● The interviewer may be someone you know.
● The interview could end with you being offered the job.

Panel interviews

Most interviews are one-on-ones or, at most, there will be two people sitting on the other side of the desk. Where you are going to be interviewed by a panel of people, you will usually be given some prior warning in your invitation to the interview, but do not rely on this.

Telephone interviews

Telephone interviews have come onto the scene in recent years and are associated with the visible market, where employers first have the task of reducing the candidates to a more manageable number. Telephone interviews are often in place of preliminary interviews. They are quick and instant and this is their appeal.

Key points to note about telephone interviews are:

● They are short, with questions rattled off at you in checklist fashion.
● The test is again one of 'broad suitability'.
● The challenge is to get across what you need to in the time available.
● The interviewer has probably got a list of calls to make, so do not expect him or her to spend any more time on you than is absolutely necessary.

Selection tests

To administer a selection test calls for a level of competency that is not present in all organizations. For this reason, you are only likely to run into one:

● in a large company where there is a professional human resources function
● where consultants are involved.

Where called for, a selection test can be put in front of you at almost any point in the procedure, i.e. at a preliminary interview or at the short-list stage. Alternatively, you may be asked to come back on a completely separate occasion.

> **Question:** How much store do employers set by selection tests? What, for example, if a candidate does well in an interview but scores poorly in a test?
>
> **Answer:** From our experience, a poor result in a test will not put an employer off a candidate they have already taken a shine to in an interview. In such circumstances, it is often the test that is blamed for throwing out a seemingly inconsistent reading.

Assessment centres

Assessment centres are whole days of interviews, panel interviews, selection tests, presentations, round-table discussions and other activities designed to show candidates in a true light and to assess their suitability. Typically, they are used where employers are planning an intake (e.g. graduates, new product sales team, etc.). Assessment centres are often run by consultants with managers from the employing company participating.

Interviewers

Just as interviews vary, so do interviewers and their styles. As a rule of thumb, the way interviewers approach the job will chiefly be determined by:

● how trained and experienced they are
● how much time and resources they have available.

Who is doing the interview?

Clearly there is a world of difference between:

● an interview conducted by a professional (e.g. a human resources specialist or a selection consultant), and

> ● one carried out by the line manager in whose area the job is based.
>
> With the former, the interview will tend to be structured and follow a defined pattern. With the latter, the questions will be more random and out of sequence. Moreover, a professional will only have a general understanding of whatever it is you do for a living, whereas the person who could be your next boss will be focused on how much you know (expect the questions to reflect this).

Finding out about interviewers

Even though it helps to see the general directions that interviewers are coming from, it still does not prepare you for individuals. What questions does Mr Bloggs of S Company like to ask? More importantly, what answers is he looking for? At the same time does Mr Bloggs have any peculiarities or quirks?

What can consultants tell you?

Many jobs are sourced through consultants of one sort or another and, as remarked previously, these consultants are often storehouses of information on employers, including their interview methods; for instance:

● any favourite questions they like to ask
● what's behind the questions
● how best to answer
● any likes and dislikes.

> Many consultants will have dealt with employers over long periods, hence they have often picked up feedback from candidates who have been for interview before.
>
> Reminder: do not fight shy of picking consultants' brains. There is usually a good pay-off for them if you are successful in getting the job.

Tapping into your networks

Your networks are another good source of information on interviewers. Has anyone you know attended an interview in the past with this particular interviewer? If so, what can they tell you about the way the interview went? Do they have any tips for you? Alternatively, can they put you in touch with someone better placed to give you a few insights?

Small worlds

This advice underlines an important point about networking in practice – we all tend to operate in small worlds, the boundaries to which are determined by:

● the geographical areas in which we work (or have worked in the past)
● our own particular occupations or professions.

Within these small worlds, people tend to know one another: paths cross and you usually do not have to go very far before you find someone who can give you some helpful information. The key to networks is to use them.

Researching employers

Finding out more about employers has two purposes:

1 It helps you deal with the question 'What do you know about us?' if it should happen to come up.
2 It will enable you to start to assess the organization as a prospective employer.

Sources of information

You can glean employer information by:

● looking at the employer's website
● paying a visit to the public library
● if the employer is a public company, obtaining a copy of their report and accounts.

Do not, however, overlook the following:

● Your networks (remember those small worlds – someone you know is almost bound to have some information that will be useful to you).
● People who work in certain fields, such as sales, credit control, mergers and acquisitions are often mines of information on companies.
● Any consultants who have been involved in selection.

What do you know about us?

The key to dealing with this favourite interview question is to keep the answer concise. Tell the interviewer:

● what you know (keep it to three or four sentences)
● where you got the information, i.e. to show what you have done to find out more about them
● that it sounds like the kind of organization you would like to work for.

 TIP *The mistake – and plenty make it – is to answer the 'What do you know about us?' question with a long, pre-prepared speech . Don't. It will not do anything to enhance your chances and, more to the point, it will eat into precious interview time (time that could be better spent on getting across the strong areas in your application).*

Before you go

What else do you need to think about before you go to an interview?

Diary planning

You will have no idea in advance about:

● how long the interview will last
● whether the interviews will be running on time.

Therefore, do not put pressure on yourself by committing to other engagements, such as picking up children or being back at work by a certain time. It will not be your fault if the interviews are running half an hour late, but equally it will not do much for your chances if you have to excuse yourself halfway through.

Check your journey time

We saw on Monday that good first impressions are a vital part of any interview, hence the importance of ensuring that you arrive on time. Do a dummy run beforehand and check:

● how long it will take you
● whether parking is available.

> If your interview is in a city centre or anywhere else where parking may be difficult, give consideration to:
>
> ● getting a taxi
> ● getting someone to give you a lift.
>
> With an interview, nothing is worse than getting into a panic at the last minute because you think you are going to be late.

Visual aids

With some occupations (e.g. designers), it is normal practice to take a portfolio of your work to interviews. Points to bear in mind are:

- Do not overdo it. Interviewers will look at your portfolio out of politeness and, if it is bulky, this will take precious minutes out of your interview time (precious minutes that could be put to better use).
- Pick out a few examples only and the criterion you should use in making this selection is the relevance of the material to the job for which you are applying.

> Interviews that do not finish the course because they run out of time are a problem, particularly with preliminary interviews where it is customary for candidates to be seen in a procession – one after the other. Be aware of this problem. Do not put interviewers in the position where they have to rush things at the end. Do not find the interviewers saying goodbye to you before you have managed to put your most important messages across.

Even if you are not a designer, visual aids are still worth a thousand words and nowhere more so than at an interview. Why?

- Visuals can cut out the need for long verbal descriptions and save on interview time.

- Visuals will help you when it comes to dealing with professional interviewers (e.g. human resources specialists or consultants who may not be totally familiar with all the intricacies of your line of work).

In short, having visual aids is another example of being 'employer friendly'. Examples of useful visual aids are:

- photographs of projects you have worked on
- sales information or product catalogues
- company brochures and other public relations material
- press releases, especially those that relate to your key achievements.

 As you move from job to job, try to accumulate visual aids that you can use for interviews. Keep them in a safe place.

Revisit the advertisement

Always keep a copy of any job advertisement that you reply to, so that you can look at it again before you go for an interview. Long periods of time can sometimes elapse between an ad appearing in the paper and the interview list being drawn up. Reminding yourself of what was in the ad is a good way to remind yourself of the strong areas of your application (the messages you need to get across).

Revisit other documents

Remind yourself what you put in:

- your CV
- your letter of application
- any forms you have filled in.

This is to avoid saying something at an interview that completely contradicts information you have given elsewhere. Remember Monday's lesson – your credibility could be at stake.

Summary

Today you have taught yourself that the right way to go about interviews is to do your homework first. You have taught yourself that:

● some interviews are fitted into time slots where you need to be mindful of the need to get your key messages across before the time runs out

● some interviews are designed to assess 'broad suitability' rather than decide who to offer the job to.

For example, an interview with someone you have known through the trade for the past 15 years will be very different from an interview with a professional selection consultant who is a complete stranger to you. Similarly, an interview where you are one of a number of people being seen will be very different from one where you are the only candidate. The key is to take these differences into account in the preparations you make.

Today you have also taught yourself to think through how you are going to get to the interview and the importance of arriving on time. On Monday you taught yourself the importance of making good early impressions. Today you taught yourself that turning up late for an interview is a bad start from which you may find it impossible to recover.

Finally, today you have taught yourself what information you need to revisit before you go for an interview. In particular you have seen why it is important that you look again at what you said about yourself in any documents you have already submitted to the employer including your CV and application form.

Fact-check (answers at the back)

1. When is it likely you will be asked to attend a preliminary interview first?
   a) When there are a lot of applicants ❑
   b) When consultants are advising on the appointment ❑
   c) When there is more than one position to fill ❑
   d) When the position is relatively junior ❑

2. What will the interviewer be seeking to establish at a preliminary interview?
   a) Who is offered the job ❑
   b) How many of the applicants drop out ❑
   c) Broad suitability ❑
   d) How applicants react when they are put under pressure ❑

3. What is a short-list?
   a) An interview list where there is only one candidate ❑
   b) Candidates held in reserve in case the preferred candidate does not take the job ❑
   c) Candidates who are good in most respects but who are short on experience ❑
   d) Preferred candidates who are brought back for a second interview ❑

4. What are assessment centres?
   a) Places where you to learn about interviews ❑
   b) Places where interviewers are trained ❑
   c) Whole days of activities designed to pick out suitable candidates ❑
   d) Rooms used for interviews ❑

5. With preliminary interviews, what is the most common mistake that candidates make?
   a) Arriving late ❑
   b) Talking too much then finding the interview runs out of time ❑
   c) Not talking enough ❑
   d) Not paying enough attention to their personal appearance ❑

6. Before going to a preliminary interview why is it important to revisit the copies you kept of your application letter, CV and application form?
   a) So you can answer questions you are asked at the interview without having to refer to anything ❑
   b) So you can remind yourself what you said and in this way make sure that at the interview you do not destroy your credibility by contradicting yourself ❑
   c) So you can put interviewers right who misquote you ❑
   d) To boost your confidence by reminding yourself how brilliant you are ❑

7. When do you need to be prepared for a first interview that ends with you being offered the job?

a) When the interviewer knows you ❏

b) When you are the only applicant ❏

c) When your CV is brilliant ❏

d) When the interview lasts a long time ❏

8. You are invited to an interview in a busy city centre where parking could be a problem. What do you do?

a) Phone up and say you could be late ❏

b) Worry about it when it happens ❏

c) Go on your bike ❏

d) Get a taxi or get someone to give you a lift ❏

9. What is the point of taking visual aids to an interview?

a) So you can give the interviewer a presentation ❏

b) To take attention away from weak areas in your application ❏

c) Where it might make it easier and quicker to explain ❏

d) To make you more employer friendly ❏

10. What should you expect when an interview is being conducted by an HR professional?

a) Tougher questions ❏

b) A more structured approach ❏

c) An interview that lasts longer ❏

d) A less friendly approach ❏

SUNDAY

MONDAY

TUESDAY

WEDNESDAY

THURSDAY

FRIDAY

SATURDAY

Handling
questions

Teach yourself today what to do when you are sitting in the hot seat and questions are being fired at you. Teach yourself how to handle the questions and, at the same time, what you have to do to make sure that what you want to say about yourself comes out.

Teach yourself how to manage the time frames into which interviews are slotted so, when you get to the end, you are not left with the feeling that your best points did not come out.

Yesterday you taught yourself how interviews and interviewers differ. Today teach yourself that the questions that interviewers ask differ also. Some are predictable but with others it can sometimes be difficult to see what the interviewer is driving at.

Teach yourself today the secrets of dealing with tricky interview questions – not just how to answer them but how to answer them in a way that will bring the strong areas of your application back into focus.

Teach yourself today the right and wrong ways to answer some of the more obvious questions that will be put to you. See how some answers could put the kiss of death on your application.

Finally, teach yourself today how to deal with interviewers who are inexperienced and who do not ask the right questions. See how sometimes you have to make up for their lack of experience.

Appreciating the time frames

Coming out of an interview feeling that you have not put your best points across is an experience many candidates share. Usually the blame is placed on the interviewer for either not asking the right questions or not giving the interview sufficient time.

> ### Important
> The responsibility for getting your messages across rests entirely on you. This is all part of the principle of taking control.

How long have you got?

You may not know in advance how much time the interviewer has allowed you. Is it an hour? Or is it just 30 minutes? In some cases, you may be told at the start how long an interview is going to last but, more often than not, you will not have the foggiest idea. The first inkling you will get that time has run out will be when the closing signals begin to flash at you – the signals that the interviewer is trying to wrap it up.

Where time frames are important

There will be greatest pressure on time if interviews are done in strings, one after the other. The next candidate will be waiting outside and the interviewer will be anxious to move on. What is more, allowing an interview to over run will have a knock-on effect on the rest of the interviewer's day.

Therefore, he or she will make strenuous efforts to ensure that this does not happen.

> Preliminary interviews, where many candidates are seen, are often done in strings. Here, you must make the greatest allowance for getting your messages across in the time available.

Telephone interviews

While phoning a batch of candidates and asking them a series of questions will not necessarily be done to a fixed timetable, there is nevertheless pressure on the interviewer to get through the list of calls as quickly as possible. Hence, the time allotted to each call will be limited. Once again, the challenge is for the candidate to get their main messages across in the limited time available.

How to avoid running out of time

With the clock ticking against you in some interviews, you must:

- always keep your answers to questions relevant, short and concise (do not chatter on)
- never take over interviews, for example, by saying, 'Shall I tell you about myself?' and launching into a 15-minute oral version of your CV
- watch out for closing signs (such as the interviewer getting fidgety or glancing at their watch). Closing signs are the signal to pull the emergency lever and impart any remaining main messages in a hurry.

The importance of first and last impressions

There are two important parts to any interview. One is at the beginning when the halo effects form. The other is at the end because this is the impression of you that the interviewer takes away – the one that will be decisive when it comes to picking the short-list or deciding who gets the job.

First impressions

Due to the importance of halo effects, you have been working on your first (or early) impressions ever since you put in your application. You paid attention to the presentation of your CV, your letter of application and any forms you filled in.

You now want to carry over these same good impressions into your interview.

Arriving on time

The classic bad start to any interview is arriving late (a bad start from which it is difficult to recover). Note the advice given yesterday about planning your journey.

Question: What if the unexpected happens – if, for example, your train is cancelled or you run into a tailback on the motorway?

Answer: Get on the phone straight away (always have a mobile phone on you when you go to an interview). Tell the interviewer:

- that you are running late
- the reason
- when you expect to arrive.

This gives the interviewer the option to cancel the interview (giving you another appointment). It avoids:

- you and your late arrival being to blame for the whole programme of interviews running late in a string of interviews

> ● your interview being cut short to prevent delays to other interviews.

Appearance

If the interviewer has never seen you before, your appearance will clearly be a decisive factor in any first impressions you make. This is why you must always pay attention to what you wear for interviews and to items such as personal grooming. This, you will remember, is a subject we looked at on Monday, when we considered the quality of the image you project.

What to wear

Once upon a time it was an unwritten rule that you put on your best clothes when you went for an interview. However, is this the case today, when people are far more casual about what they wear for work? Indeed by overdressing for an interview, could you come across as formal and starchy, i.e. not give a good impression?

The clothes you choose for an interview should be:

● consistent with the job you are applying for
● smart (even casual clothes can look smart)

- clean
- comfortable
- a reflection of you.

> This last bullet point is important because the clothes you choose, the colours and styles you put together and the accessories you wear all convey something of you that interviewers:
>
> - notice
> - latch on to.
>
> In this way, clothes become the catalyst around which the engagement factors start to form (the factors which draw employers to individual applicants and which we drew your attention to on Monday).

It is interesting to note that, at the end of a string of interviews, interviewers often bring candidates back to mind by reference to something they wore, for example, 'The girl with the marcasite earrings', 'The bloke with the nice blue tie', etc. These points of recollection are important because otherwise candidates' faces all tend to blur into one.

Last impressions

Just as important as first impressions are those you leave behind as you walk out of the door.

> A *faux pas* in the middle of an interview has a chance:
>
> - to correct itself
> - of being overlooked because of a good first impression (the halo effect).
>
> However, a *faux pas* at the end of an interview will:
>
> - stay fresh in the memory
> - occur at the point in the interview furthest removed from the good first impression, i.e. when the halo effect is at its weakest.

Talking yourself out of the job

Sometimes an interviewer will ask you at the end of an interview if there is anything you want to add – a question that can have you scratching your head for something to say.

If you succeeded in registering your important messages during the course of the interview, you will not need to add anything. Do not, whatever you do, launch into a long ramble about nothing and put your foot in it at the same time. Remember that it is very easy to put the kiss of death on an interview in its closing moments. Often the best bet is to keep quiet.

Spotting what is behind the questions

An interview will typically follow a question and answer format. Nevertheless, as we saw yesterday, the questions thrown at you will vary widely. They depend upon:

● the kind of interview
● the interviewer and his or her background, experience and quirks.

Some questions clearly call for straightforward factual answers, whereas others have you puzzling about where they are leading.

Listen to questions

Do not do the politician's trick of answering a different question from the one you have been asked because:

● it will waste precious interview time (the interviewer will have to put the question to you again)
● the interviewer will find it irritating.

Listen to questions carefully. It sounds obvious but it is surprising how many candidates develop cloth ears as soon as they sit down in the hot seat.

Are you suitable for the job?

So much has been written about interviews that it is easy to forget their purpose. Broadly speaking an employer is seeking to find out:

● Can you do the job?
● Will you fit in?

Are you competent to do the job?

With jobs sourced on the invisible market, your competence is not such a big issue. Where, for example, you have been approached or you have sourced a job by tapping into your networks, the people interviewing you will probably have some knowledge of your track record. Indeed, the fact that you are there can be taken as an indicator that what they know about you is good. All you need to do now is:

● confirm that opinion
● not do anything to raise doubts.

However, your competence is an issue if the interviewer does not know you, i.e. the typical visible market situation where you are just a name on the interview list. This is where you have a task on your hands. You need to bear in mind the following:

- Remember that employers are not impressed by candidates who give glowing descriptions of themselves. They have heard it all before.
- Professional interviewers (e.g. consultants, human resources managers) will not be over-familiar with the ins and outs of what you do and you need to be interviewer friendly by avoiding technical jargon or losing them in long, detailed descriptions. Going back to yesterday's lesson, your visual aids could help.
- Most information assimilated at an interview is taken on trust. You give some information in answer to a question and the interviewer believes you – unless they have reason to do otherwise. The point at issue here is your credibility – you will not get anywhere in an interview if the person on the other side of the desk feels you are being economical with the truth. In addition, the commonest way that applicants sow seeds of doubt about themselves is by introducing contradictions between what they say at interviews and what they have written in CVs and so forth. Revisit CVs, application forms, etc. before you go to the interview.

Will you fit in?

With so much accent these days on team working, a concern in every employer's mind is whether you will fit in with the rest of the team or whether you could turn out to be a square peg in a round hole and be a thorn in their sides.

When answering any questions put to you at an interview, always emphasize the team effort if talking about your present and previous jobs. Do not make it sound as if turning the business around from massive losses was something you did single-handedly because, apart from anything else, no one will believe you. Here are a couple of tips:

- *When talking about past achievements, always mention the contribution of colleagues.*
- *Use 'we' and 'us' in your descriptions, rather than 'I' and 'me'.*

What makes you tick?

Part of the assessment of whether you are a potential square peg in a round hole is finding out what drives you. Why did you choose the paths you took? Why did you leave Company A to join Company B? Why did you take time out to do an MBA? Why did you decide to work in Japan for four years? It is answers to questions like these that give interviewers insights into what motivates you and whether it is consistent with being a good team player.

Because of the disruptive effect it can have on the workings of a team, employers are anxious to avoid taking on the kind of people who grumble about everything and are never satisfied. Therefore, you need to be very careful about the reasons you give for leaving jobs. Here are a few examples of the right and wrong ways of saying the same things:

Wrong	Right
They paid me peanuts.	I decided to look for a job where my talents would be better rewarded.
The training opportunities were rubbish.	I wanted to work for an organization where I could develop my skills and advance my career.
My boss didn't have a clue.	I needed to work for more professional people.

The trick is to turn the negative into the positive – to focus attention on what you want for the future, rather than on problems attached to what you are doing now.

Allowing for interviewers' omissions

An important part of keeping control of interviews is having some fail-safe systems to take account of:

● poor interviewers
● interviewers who do not give themselves enough time
● interviewers who are distracted by interruptions.

Inexperienced interviewers and those in a rush sometimes omit to ask all the questions. They get half the story and then they move on. In the example below, the candidate is being interviewed for a job where knowledge of certain types of software (XXX) is a requirement, although the candidate is unaware of this because it was not mentioned in the advertisement.

> **Interviewer:** I see you've been with Bloggs & Co for the last two and a half years. What software do you use?
>
> **Candidate:** YYY.
>
> **Interviewer:** What about XXX?
>
> **Candidate:** There's talk about buying a package, but as far as I know no decision has been taken.

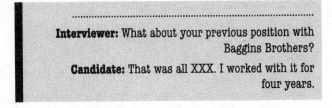

> **Interviewer:** What about your previous position with Baggins Brothers?
>
> **Candidate:** That was all XXX. I worked with it for four years.

The dotted line in the script indicates where some interviewers would end the interrogation. As a consequence, they would wrongly form the view that the candidate has no experience with XXX.

Where a particular line of questioning is followed, try to spot what is behind it ('Why am I being asked about XXX?'). If the questions peter out before the interviewer has got the full story, seize the initiative and take control. See to it that the interviewer goes away with the right facts. Note: lines of questioning such as these often reveal hidden selection criteria. Here, using the same example as above, is how the candidate could have seized the initiative:

> **Interviewer:** I see you've been with Bloggs & Co for the last two and a half years. What software do you use?
>
> **Candidate:** YYY.
>
> **Interviewer:** What about XXX?
>
> **Candidate:** There's talk about buying a package, but as far as I know no decision has been taken. But in my previous job with Baggins Brothers I worked with XXX for four years.

Questions that do not get asked

Another type of question that does not get asked is one the interviewer finds difficult or embarrassing or that could give the impression of prying.

An example is the candidate who is a single parent with two small children. The interviewer will be quick to spot the potential conflicts that could arise but may hesitate about asking questions that could be seen as intruding into the candidate's private life. Here the candidate needs to consider saying something that will help put the interviewer's mind at rest, e.g. about child minding arrangements.

Pre-emptive strikes

Sometimes it is necessary to put yourself in employers' shoes and see their concerns. Where there is something in your life that could come into conflict with the demands of a job then, rather than leave employers to draw their own conclusions, take control and clear up the concern.

Make sure you get your messages across

Your main task in an interview is to steer the discussion so that as much time as possible is spent talking about the strong areas in your application. To an extent, this will happen naturally. Interviewers will focus on what interests them and all you need do is sit back and answer the questions. They will also have your CV, letter of application or application form in front of them. These documents will highlight your strong areas (you have made sure of this). In short you have:

● set the agenda for your interview
● ensured that it is favourable to you
● taken control.

When to hit the emergency button

If, however, you sense the interview is about to close and you have not managed to register one of your strong areas, it is time to hit the emergency button.

An occasion may still present itself to insert the vital missing piece of information. For example, the interviewer may ask you at the end of the interview if you want to add anything. Alternatively, you may have to say something like, 'Oh by the way, I noticed you mentioned XYZ experience in your ad and I just wanted to draw your attention to the time I spent with Bodgitt & Associates. I worked with XYZ practically the whole time I was there.'

Summary

What you have taught yourself today is that the responsibility for getting the right messages across at an interview rests on you and nobody else.

While this is easily said, it can be difficult to achieve especially in situations where interviewers are in a rush or where they don't have a clue about what questions to ask. Today you have taught yourself to deal with these situations without going to the other extreme and taking over interviews (the best way of ensuring that interviewers switch off and stop listening).

Today you have taught yourself that agendas for interviews are usually dictated by what interviewers have in front of them. In most cases this will consist of:

● your CV
● your application form
● any letters you have written in support of your application.

This week you have already taught yourself to use documents such as these as vehicles for getting your messages across and in particular the strong areas of your application. If you have done the job properly, you will find therefore that most of the questions you are asked are the ones you want to be asked.

SUNDAY
MONDAY
TUESDAY
WEDNESDAY
THURSDAY
FRIDAY
SATURDAY

Fact-check (answers at the back)

1. Where is awareness of time frames important?
   a) Interviews done in a procession, one interview after the next ❑
   b) Interviews done in the evening after work ❑
   c) Interviews for junior positions ❑
   d) Interviews done over the phone ❑

2. What is it important to achieve when interviews are done to tight timescales?
   a) Get to know the interviewer ❑
   b) Get your important messages across ❑
   c) Get information on the salary ❑
   d) Get out as quickly as possible ❑

3. You are on your way to an interview when the traffic comes to a standstill on the motorway. Soon it becomes apparent that you are in for a long delay meaning, at best, you will be arriving for the interview three-quarters of an hour late. What do you do?
   a) Forget the interview. Turn round at the next junction and go back home ❑
   b) Arrive late and apologize ❑
   c) Get on the phone straight away, explain the situation and leave it to the employer to decide what to do ❑
   d) Get on the phone and cancel ❑

4. An interview goes well but at the end the interviewer asks you if you have anything to add. You think you have covered everything but what is it best to say?
   a) Talk about whatever comes into your head ❑
   b) Repeat the information that you have already given ❑
   c) Tell the interviewer how brilliant you are ❑
   d) Nothing apart from saying thank you and that you are interested in the job ❑

5. What will you gain from listening to questions properly and answering the ones you have been asked?
   a) Better use of interview time ❑
   b) Less chance of contradicting yourself ❑
   c) Better rapport with the interviewer ❑
   d) A place on the short-list ❑

6. What is the best way of convincing interviewers you are telling them the truth?
   a) By telling them what an honest person you are ❑
   b) By not contradicting yourself ❑
   c) By talking about your religious beliefs ❑
   d) By looking them in the eye ❑

7. What do you do about interviewers who do not ask you the right questions (questions that would enable you to give a fuller account of your attributes and experience)?
a) Write the interview off ☐
b) Blame the interviewer if you don't get the job ☐
c) Make a pre-emptive strike ☐
d) Walk out ☐

8. Why are interviewers always interested in the reasons why you left jobs?
a) It tells them about your motivation ☐
b) It puts you on the spot ☐
c) It tells them how much pressure you can handle ☐
d) They are looking to see if you have ever had the sack ☐

9. When is it best to tell the interviewer how brilliant you are?
a) At the beginning of the interview ☐
b) At the end ☐
c) Both **a** and **b** ☐
d) You don't ☐

10. An interviewer keeps having to stop to take telephone calls. Do you:
a) ask if you can come back at a more convenient time? ☐
b) walk out in protest? ☐
c) be patient and put up with it? ☐
d) tell the interviewer you object and suggest his/her phone is switched off? ☐

SATURDAY

In the last few

Teach yourself today what to do when you get put on the short-list. The first interview went well and now the employer wants to take another look at you. The job is almost in your grasp but there is just one last hoop to get through.

Teach yourself today to consider what it means to be on a short-list and how to deal with the task that still remains. OK, the employer liked what they saw first time round but, unless you are lucky, you will not be the only face still left in the frame. There will be others and the others will be like you – candidates who came through the test of broad suitability and who will have credentials that are not dissimilar to yours. What you are seeking therefore is something to distance you from the rest and today you will teach yourself how to go about finding it.

Today you will also teach yourself what to do if you end up as the number two choice. On the face of it there are no prizes for coming second but today you will teach yourself that this is not necessarily the case.

Getting on the short-list and what this means

In the normal context, getting on the short-list means passing the preliminary interview vetting stage and being amongst the chosen few that the employer has decided to bring back for a second showing. It means also that:

- you have passed the test of broad suitability
- everything else you have done so far is OK.

Getting to meet the decision makers

If consultants and human resources specialists have run the show up to now, the short-list stage could be where they step aside and let the real decision makers take over – the people who will have the final say on whether you are going to get the job or not. In other words, you will have to stand up to a completely fresh round of scrutiny by different people. It does not necessarily follow that these people will take the same view of you that the first interviewer took. Indeed, there are many instances where candidates have come out of preliminary interviews with flying colours only to fall flat on their faces when they got on to the short-list.

Competition

In terms of quantity, the competition you face when you get on to a short-list is less formidable because of the simple fact that a large number of candidates will have been rejected already. In terms of quality, however, the reverse applies. It pays to remember that the candidates you are up against now will be those who have also impressed – from here on it is going to get much tougher.

Warning – do not relax

A temptation when you get on to a short-list is to feel that you have done the hard part and the rest should be plain sailing. Do not succumb to this temptation. Because of the competition, you need to be on your mettle when you reach the final stages of any selection process. Feeling you are almost home and dry will not help you when it comes to giving your best performance.

Seeing the same interviewer again

Selection procedures do not follow a standard pattern and so there is always the possibility that your second (short-list) interview will be with the same interviewer. This is more likely to happen where a human resources specialist or consultant is not involved at the first stage. For example, where a manager is handling the recruitment exercise without any professional help and the purpose of the second interview will be:

- to confirm a view already taken at the first interview
- to view the cream of the candidates on an occasion when there is more time available to spend with them.

Fine points

It is interesting that final selection decisions in competitive employment situations are often made on very fine points. For instance, it is not unusual at the end of a series of interviews and re-interviews for an employer to find that he or she is faced with a number of candidates who would all be perfectly capable of doing the job. Who to choose? This is where it gets difficult and the balance can be tipped in a candidate's favour by relatively minor items in his or her portfolio. Even here, employers can still be pushed to make a decision.

Getting turned down

Nothing is more disappointing than attending several interviews and doing selection tests, to discover at the end of it all that the job is offered to someone else. You find it hard to understand why you were not chosen and you rack your brains searching for the reasons. Did you commit some awful gaffe at the final interview? Or was there something wrong with the way you presented yourself?

Tormenting yourself with questions like these is largely pointless. If you got on a short-list for a good job, where there was an abundance of applicants, then you did well and this is the way you should view it. The message to you now is 'keep going' because you are getting it right and sooner or later a good offer will come your way. The fact that you got pipped to the post on this occasion is neither here nor there. In any case, the final selection decision was probably made on some very minor point and it would be a mistake to view your rejection as a signal to start overhauling your whole approach.

Arriving at the final decision

There is no guarantee that a selection decision will be made once the short-list interviews have taken place. The employer may decide to bring some of the candidates back for another showing (a short short-list). Alternatively, they may pick out one candidate who they prefer to the rest and parade them in front of someone like the chief executive (a 'rubber-stamping' exercise). The possibilities and combinations are almost endless.

What the employers like about you

The fact that you have got this far tells you that there is something the company likes about you. This is a useful place to start when it comes to planning how to play a second interview. What they like about you is what you need to keep the interview focused upon. Conversely, anything that could give the company cause for second thoughts (a weak area), needs to be scrupulously avoided.

Keeping the engagement factors working

Remember that an important part of the strategy of taking control and steering applications to successful outcomes is to encourage a bond to develop between you and your prospective employer – a bond that:

● grows stronger as the selection process moves forward
● enhances your chances of becoming the preferred candidate at the end.

Why you got on the short-list

Usually there are a few clues to why an employer decides to ask you back for a second interview. The way the discussion went at the first interview, where interest was shown in specific areas of your portfolio and what questions were asked are all useful pointers to where the focus of interest in you lies. Coupled with which, you will already have a few insights into what qualities the employer is looking for – insights gained, for example, from reading the advertisement for the job or from information passed on to you by people such as consultants.

Getting feedback from consultants

If consultants have had a hand in putting you forward for a job, they are a very useful source of post-interview feedback. They will make it their business to contact the employer soon after first interviews to find out how you got on. If the verdict on you is favourable, the employer will usually tell the consultants what they found good about your application. This can then be passed on to you.

What distances you from the rest

Except by chance or if some selection method based on group interaction is used, it is unlikely you will ever get much insight into the calibre of the other candidates. Whether the competition you are up against is tough, feeble or somewhere in the middle is, in most cases, something you will only be able to speculate about. Given, however, that final selection decisions are often made on very fine distinctions between candidates, clearly it would be helpful to you to have some idea of where you may have an advantage over the others before your second interview.

How do you get such information?

Needless to say you cannot obtain information on other candidates, but you can make some intelligent guesses. For example, if you have been in the trade for the past 20 years, it is a safe bet that you will rate highly against the other candidates when it comes to having contacts and knowing your way around. During the second interview you can make sure:

- these facts do not go unnoticed
- you tell the interviewer how you see your trade experience as an important asset to you if you should be fortunate enough to get the job, i.e. plant the idea in their head that trade experience should rank highly on the list of selection criteria.

Handling short-list interviews

Just like preliminary interviews, short-list interviews can take practically any form. At one end of the spectrum, they can be a one-on-one interview with the interviewer who saw you the first time. At the other extreme, they can be a full-blown panel session with you sitting in the lonely space on one side of a long table confronted by faces you have never seen before.

Characteristics of short-list interviews

Given their diversity, it is hard to make generalizations about short-list interviews and the form they will take. However, the following points are worth noting:

- With fewer candidates to see, time constraints are less of an issue. Either longer time slots will be allocated to each interview or candidates will be seen on separate occasions instead of in a string of interviews. Alternatively, the interviews will be allowed to overrun because the knock-on effects will be less serious.
- The purpose of the interview is to decide who to offer the job to (rather than to assess 'broad suitability').

Keep up the good work

A short-list interview is very much a case of carrying on where you left off at the end of the first interview. In other words, you have done well up to now so keep going (keep up the good work). Focus on what got you this far and aim to give the employers more of the same.

Will anything help you?

● Remember the engagement factors and do your best to be you (in a close-run match, the job could be offered to the candidate who the employer feels most comfortable with and this is unlikely to be someone who comes across as a cardboard cut-out).

● Do not do anything that could put dents in your credibility. Again look at your CV and application form before you go to the interview, so that you are fully briefed on everything you have said about yourself. In addition, try to recall the answers to questions you gave at the first interview, so that you do not fall into the trap of giving conflicting information.

● Remember the need to put clear space between you and the other candidates on the short-list. Do this by drawing attention to areas where you feel you may have the advantage.

Where professionals could come to your rescue

Where professionals (e.g. consultants, human resources specialists) have been involved in the early stages of selection, it is not unusual to find that they 'sit in' at the short-list stage. They may take a back seat, while most of the grilling is done by the line manager responsible for making the appointment. Where this happens, the professional will tend to have a vested interest in making sure that you come across in your best possible light because it shows that they made the right decision to put you on the short-list. This could include coming to your rescue if you start to flounder. Prick your ears up, therefore, if the professional who short-listed you asks you a question. It could be a nudge to repair an omission or some damage you have inflicted on yourself unknowingly.

Post-interview availability

Do not go off on holiday or do anything else that could render you uncontactable in the period immediately following short-list interview. If a holiday is pre-booked (i.e. unavoidable), make sure you tell the employer and give your date of return. Do not risk being away when the employer tries to put the job offer in your hands. Keep your phone switched on while you are away and check your missed calls and voicemail messages.

When you are the number two choice

Selection exercises do not always go smoothly. One of the following may happen:

● The selected candidate turns down the offer.
● The selected candidate is bought off by his or her present employer.

- The selected candidate fails to start.
- The selected candidate starts but it is already apparent that they are a mismatch, i.e. a selection mistake.

Effectively, this puts the employer with the vacancy back to square one. They have the unappealing prospect of having to go through the whole time- and effort-consuming process of recruitment all over again. Small wonder, therefore, that most employers put in this situation will react by revisiting the short-list. Was there an acceptable number two?

If this happens and you are the number two choice, then all well and good. Nevertheless, employers do not always do what seems obvious. The reasons are as follows:

- It does not occur to them.
- They have already turned the number two choice down and they find it too hard to go back.
- The number two choice will know that he or she is the number two choice and some employers will view this as a bad start.
- They assume that the number two choice will not be interested because of being turned down or because of the passage of time.

Keep your face in the frame

When you have come close to getting a job (e.g. you have been on the short-list), it pays to keep your face in the frame to allow for:

- the selected candidate not starting
- the employer not feeling it is appropriate to revisit the short-list.

Timing your move is critical. Here is what you must do:

- When you receive the letter advising you that your application was unsuccessful, count off five working days and then write or e-mail the employer. Say how disappointing it was to hear that you did not get the job, but thank them for the opportunity and express your continuing interest should any similar post arise in future. This puts you in the position of being the most visible (accessible) alternative candidate if the number one choice turns the offer down.
- A month or so later ring the employer. Remind them who you are and say that you called to find out if the position had now been filled. You can add that the job interested you and that it was disappointing when you did not get it, etc. You are now in a good position if the number one choice has not started or if he or she is there but performing poorly.

Being employer friendly again

Breaking down barriers by being proactive is all part of being employer friendly. In this instance, it could mean the difference between you being offered the job and seeing it tossed back onto the open market where it will attract competition again.

Do not queer your pitch

Getting a rejection letter after you have been put through a process of applications, selection tests, interviews, re-interviews, taking time off work and footing the bill for petrol and fares is upsetting, to say the least. Furthermore, this upset can quite easily turn into anger. The upshot is that candidates phone employers, write to them or send e-mails to vent their feelings. Alternatively, they may present the employer with a bill for the money they have spent on travelling or, in some cases, to cover their loss of earnings.

Why is this bad?

Apart from achieving little (a waste of energy), such outbursts undo all the good work you have done up to now. This will work against you if:

● you are the number two choice and the number one choice turns the job down

● another equally interesting opportunity arises in the near future and, before advertising, the employer decides to look through previous candidates.

The message?

Keep your image intact. Do not do anything that will queer your pitch.

Summary

Today you have taught yourself not to see getting on a short-list as a case of 'job done'. There is still a long way to go and, in many ways, the hardest part is about to come.

Today you have taught yourself what to do when you get invited back for another interview. Here you have taught yourself to see that when this happens you face a fresh challenge – one in which you will be up against people who, in most cases, will be just as good as you and from whom you are only separated by minor points.

Today you have taught yourself to focus on these minor points and to make a few intelligent guesses on where you could have the edge on the other candidates. You have taught yourself to direct the interview into areas where you may have the edge (another example of 'taking control').

All being well you can now look forward to being offered the job but, if you are not, you have taught yourself today that getting as far as you did calls for a pat on the back not an inquest into where you went wrong.

Fact-check (answers at the back)

1. What does it mean when you are invited back for another interview?
   a) They want to offer you the job ❏
   b) It could mean anything ❏
   c) The first interview went well ❏
   d) They have forgotten what you said at the first interview and need to see you again ❏

2. Why is it important not to relax the effort when you get on a short-list?
   a) The questions will get tougher ❏
   b) There is more chance of you making a slip-up ❏
   c) You will be up against tougher competition ❏
   d) The interviewer will have to decide who gets the job, i.e. higher standards will apply ❏

3. When there are a number of candidates on the short-list who are equally capable of doing the job, what is the final selection decision likely to be based on?
   a) Tossing a coin ❏
   b) Fine points (minor differences between candidates) ❏
   c) Who is asking for the lowest salary ❏
   d) Hidden criteria ❏

4. What should you do if you are going on holiday straight after a short-list interview?
   a) Make sure you tell the employer ❏
   b) Keep your phone switched on ❏
   c) Make sure you check for missed calls and voicemail messages ❏
   d) All three ❏

5. What is it best to do when you get turned down after going to a short-list interview?
   a) Nothing ❏
   b) Send the employer an e-mail telling them they have made the wrong decision ❏
   c) Send the employer an e-mail to thank them for the opportunity and express your interest if any similar positions should arise in the future ❏
   d) Put in a claim for the expenses you incurred travelling to the interview ❏

6. Why is it important not to queer the pitch with employers who turn you down?
   a) You could be applying to them again for a different job ❏
   b) The candidate they picked may decide to turn the offer down or fail to start ❏
   c) a and b ❏
   d) Don't know ❏

7. How can you find out what you did right at the first interview?
a) By phoning the employer and asking for some feedback ❑
b) (where a recruitment consultant put you forward) By asking the recruitment consultant for feedback ❑
c) From the way the discussion went at the first interview (where the interviewer's interest in you seemed to be focused) ❑
d) There is no way of finding out ❑

8. Who will be interviewing you when you get on a short-list?
a) The same person who interviewed you first time ❑
b) Someone different ❑
c) It will depend on the employer ❑
d) A panel of interviewers ❑

9. After a short-list interview you are asked back for a third time. What do you read into this?
a) You have got the job ❑
b) You are the preferred candidate but they want to run you by someone higher up the ladder (e.g. the Chief Executive) ❑
c) They can't make up their minds ❑
d) They are time-wasters ❑

10. You have been for four jobs; each time you were put on the short-list but each time you were turned down. What do you need to do?
a) Keep going ❑
b) Redo your CV ❑
c) Ask a careers counsellor to tell you where you are going wrong ❑
d) Give up ❑

Surviving in tough times

It's never easy to get a job. In tough economic times, it is even harder, as there will be more applicants and fewer jobs available. You might find yourself up against candidates with much more experience, or being interviewed by managers who aren't really sure whether they can afford to hire at all. But don't be downhearted! If you remember what you've read in this book, you will be able to do everything possible to maximize your chances. Here are ten crucial tips that you can use to make sure you stand out from the crowd.

1 Think positive

When you think you are going to be up against large numbers of applicants, don't fall into the trap of writing off your chances before you start. Instead, tell yourself 'I can get that job' and go from there. See competition as a challenge, not a reason for getting down in the dumps. Think positive and rise to the task of engaging and overcoming it. Remember too there are still jobs out there and people are getting them. Think that next time it could be you.

2 Look forward not back

In hard times when jobs are thin on the ground and everyone is applying for them, bad experiences are a fact of life. The mistake is allowing these bad experiences to colour your perceptions on what is and what isn't achievable. Learn to put the past behind you. Treat each application you make as a fresh start and don't let anything that has happened to you before queer the pitch.

3 Be 'employer friendly'

Where employers are inundated with applications, candidates who can be quickly and easily contacted and who can attend interviews at times when employers want to see them will have an advantage over the rest. Whereas employers may be prepared to put themselves out when they are desperate to fill vacancies, this won't be the case when there are hundreds of applicants to choose from. For example, someone who can only attend interviews after hours or on weekends should not be too surprised to find they don't get very far.

4 If you've got a good image, use it

Not everyone has got a good track record, but if you have, make sure you use it. Remember those comfort factors. In difficult times, employers may not be sure about taking on new staff but they will feel more comfortable with someone who comes with a good recommendation. For example, if someone you've worked with before (such as one of your former bosses) is prepared to put in a good word for you then make it known to prospective employers.

5 Make a good early impression

When there are lots of faces in the frame, applicants can make themselves stand out by ensuring they make good early impressions. As you have seen from reading the book, a well-prepared CV and letter of application is where the business of making early impressions starts. The same goes for how you come across in the opening stages of an interview.

6 Use the power of you

When it comes to getting the job, the deciding factor is ultimately you. You have got to satisfy the employer not only that you can do the job but also that you will 'fit in'. But where the employer is faced with lots of candidates to choose from, engagement factors which you have learned about in the book start to figure more and more. Be ready, therefore, to use the power of you in competitive job situations. Don't underestimate its importance.

7 Get your strong points across

This hardly needs saying, but in competitive job situations where employers are faced with large numbers of applicants, it is vitally important to get your strong points across. Employers need to see the matches between what they are looking for and what you have to offer from a quick read of your letter, CV and application form (if you are asked to fill one in). Remember when there are piles of applications to look at, you will only have their attention for a short space of time. Remember, too, you don't get a second chance.

8 Think outside the box

Challenging situations sometimes call for innovative thinking. When financial constraints force employers to think twice about hiring staff, is there anything you could do to address their concerns? For example, could you offer to work for free for a few weeks or take a reduced salary? Employers may or may not take you up on the offer but, more importantly, you will have made a mark that will set you apart from other candidates. You will come across not only as 'employer friendly' but also as someone who has strong belief in themselves.

9 Don't get discouraged

Fretting over unsuccessful job applications is a waste of valuable energy, so whilst employers who don't reply and 'sorry but no' letters are not nice, you need to put them behind you as quickly as possible. Applying for hundreds of jobs and getting nowhere is normal in a recession, so don't see it as a reflection on you or your abilities. Keep going and don't get discouraged. Remember, discouragement is what leads to giving up.

10 Take from the experience

Going after jobs in times of recession is an experience in life at the sharp end where there are no soft cushions and where the realities are often harsh. However, like all experiences in life, it can teach you important lessons – for example, about how to deal with disappointment and how to keep picking yourself up and starting all over again. So while the hard knocks may feel painful, provided you keep going and building on experience you will come out better equipped for dealing with them and taking them in your stride. Remember, when times are hard, it's those who can keep going the longest who often come out the best.

Answers

Sunday: 1c; 2a; 3d; 4a; 5b; 6d; 7a; 8c; 9a, c; 10d

Monday: 1a; 2c; 3b; 4c; 5b; 6d; 7b; 8a; 9c; 10a

Tuesday: 1b; 2d; 3b; 4c; 5a; 6a; 7b; 8d; 9c; 10c

Wednesday: 1b; 2d; 3a; 4d; 5b; 6d; 7a; 8c; 9d; 10d

Thursday: 1a, b; 2c; 3d; 4c; 5b; 6b; 7a, b; 8d; 9c, d; 10b

Friday: 1a, d; 2b; 3c; 4d; 5a, c; 6b; 7c; 8a; 9d; 10c

Saturday: 1c; 2c; 3b, d; 4d; 5c; 6c; 7b, c; 8c; 9b, c; 10a

ALSO AVAILABLE IN THE 'IN A WEEK' SERIES

BODY LANGUAGE FOR MANAGEMENT ● BOOKKEEPING AND ACCOUNTING ● CUSTOMER CARE ● SPEED READING ● DEALING WITH DIFFICULT PEOPLE ● EMOTIONAL INTELLIGENCE ● FINANCE FOR NON-FINANCIAL MANAGERS ● INTRODUCING MANAGEMENT ● MANAGING YOUR BOSS ● MARKET RESEARCH ● NEURO-LINGUISTIC PROGRAMMING ● OUTSTANDING CREATIVITY ● PLANNING YOUR CAREER ● SUCCEEDING AT INTERVIEWS ● SUCCESSFUL APPRAISALS ● SUCCESSFUL ASSERTIVENESS ● SUCCESSFUL BUSINESS PLANS ● SUCCESSFUL CHANGE MANAGEMENT ● SUCCESSFUL COACHING ● SUCCESSFUL COPYWRITING ● SUCCESSFUL CVS ● SUCCESSFUL INTERVIEWING

For information about other titles in the series, please visit www.inaweek.co.uk

ALSO AVAILABLE IN THE 'IN A WEEK' SERIES

SUCCESSFUL JOB APPLICATIONS • SUCCESSFUL JOB HUNTING • SUCCESSFUL KEY ACCOUNT MANAGEMENT • SUCCESSFUL LEADERSHIP • SUCCESSFUL MARKETING • SUCCESSFUL MARKETING PLANS • SUCCESSFUL MEETINGS • SUCCESSFUL MEMORY TECHNIQUES • SUCCESSFUL MENTORING • SUCCESSFUL NEGOTIATING • SUCCESSFUL NETWORKING • SUCCESSFUL PEOPLE SKILLS • SUCCESSFUL PRESENTING • SUCCESSFUL PROJECT MANAGEMENT • SUCCESSFUL PSYCHOMETRIC TESTING • SUCCESSFUL PUBLIC RELATIONS • SUCCESSFUL RECRUITMENT • SUCCESSFUL SELLING • SUCCESSFUL STRATEGY • SUCCESSFUL TIME MANAGEMENT • TACKLING INTERVIEW QUESTIONS

For information about other titles in the series, please visit www.inaweek.co.uk

LEARN IN A WEEK,
WHAT THE EXPERTS
LEARN IN A LIFETIME

For information about other titles
in the series, please visit
www.inaweek.co.uk